TRAVELING
WITH
KIDS

TRAVELING WITH KIDS

101 Tips for a Great Trip

Jay A. Parry

Illustrated by
Kathy N. Pitt

Brite Music, Inc.

Acknowledgements

Our heartfelt appreciation to all the individuals, too numerous to mention, who submitted experiences and ideas that work to make traveling with children easier and more fun for all.

Cover design by Evan Twede
Special effects photography by Brian Twede

Printed in the United States of America

ISBN 0-944803-69-5

CONTENTS

⬭ **SECTION 4**
Time to Be Together

◇ **SECTION 5**
Air Travel Tips

⌂ **SECTION 6**
Tips for Hotel and Motel

⬭ **SECTION 7**
**How to Make the Same Trip Appeal to Tots
and Teens**

☐ **SECTION 8**
101+ Tips for a Great Trip

Traveling with Kids
101 Tips for a Great Trip

Introduction

We've all experienced the family trip:

"Kids, get in the car and don't start fighting."

"Bradley, scoot over. Mom, Bradley won't scoot over!"

"I said I get the window!"

"Dad, Jenny hit me."

"I did not!"

"Honey, I just <u>know</u> we're forgetting something."

"Mommy, can I have a drink of pop?"

Finally everyone is settled and Dad backs the car out of the driveway. But before he hits the street, two young voices cry out from the back seat, speaking almost in unison:

"When are we going to get there?" and

"I have to go to the bathroom!"

Family trips are supposed to build family togetherness. They get everybody together for a few days to enjoy each other's company and to have a fun, unique experience together. Unfortunately, it often turns out just the opposite. Everybody comes home exhausted and sick of being together, and it takes the parents a whole year (sometimes more) to get up the courage to try again.

Does it have to be that way?

Two families recently went on extended trips, one to Los Angeles, the other to Miami. Both have four kids and both seem to have a firm grip on what it takes to help kids get along. But they came back with very different reports.

The Clemsons returned with a disturbing horror story. "Robbie and Sara fought the whole way to L.A.," Betty Clemson said. "Rick played with his Space Invaders game so long I had nightmares for three nights, hearing beeps and buzzes in my sleep. After we arrived, Todd said he was too old to go to Disneyland and wanted to know why we'd made him come in the first place. Then Alan exploded and said we certainly didn't <u>make</u> anyone do anything and if Todd felt that way he could just sit in the motel all day and we'd save ourselves the price of entertaining him. That was just the beginning; by the time we got home I couldn't believe how relieved we were to have the stupid trip over with."

The Williams family traveled to Miami: "We had such a marvelous time, we hated to see it end. The day we got home we were ready to turn around and do it all over again."

What made the difference?

Janice Williams says, "We feel that if we want a family activity to be a success, we have to make it happen that way. We have to plan ahead, prepare, work it all out before we even start. When we do that, we have a wonderful time together. When we don't, things gradually (or sometimes quickly) fall apart."

A family trip really can be the year's highlight for all the members of the family, but such benefits don't happen automatically. We do have to work at it; we have to <u>make</u> it happen. This doesn't mean we have to force our trip to fit an ideal, but it does mean we <u>consciously</u> <u>create</u> the kind of experiences we want to have.

This book will help you see how <u>you</u> can do that. It can show you how to make your family trip a memory you'll cherish and an experience you'll want to repeat year after year.

The ideas in this book are all tried and true, used by real families on real trips. They include tips on:

- getting ready

- packing

- being safe and comfortable in the car

- food to take

- car sickness

- songs to sing and tapes to listen to

- games to play on the way

- using the time together to build togetherness

- traveling by air with kids

- surviving (and enjoying) a stay in a hotel or motel

- how to deal with the competing needs and desires of different age groups

- and much, much more.

Great trips take more effort than mediocre ones do. But the rewards are worth it, many times over.

Happy traveling!

Before You Go

Before You Go

Planning the Trip

How to sort through dozens of options, calm fighting children with opposing viewpoints, and plan a thousand-dollar trip when you have three hundred dollars in the bank.

Often when families plan trips, they already know exactly what they're going to do. For instance, the Bells' most recent family trip was to southern California. They knew right from the beginning that they wanted to do two things there: visit Jack, Mr. Bell's brother (and accept his invitation to stay in his home), and visit Disneyland. But sometimes the destination is open to discussion: "Hey, everybody, Dad's going to take a week off work and we're all going to go on a trip! Any ideas?"

How can you make the most of planning?

Remember two ideas:

First, the more everyone gets involved in the planning, the more excited everyone will be about the trip.

Second, everyone will have a better time if you plan activities with the individual needs and interests of all family members in mind.

Planning in Action

The Steve Rice family always plans things together. Right now, they're planning a trip to New Orleans, and this is the third "meeting" they've had together to decide what would make the trip more fun. Let's watch:

"Okay, last time we decided New Orleans is the destination," Dad says. "Do you have your assignments ready?"

"I do," says Jim.

"Me, too. I found some good stuff," Heather says.

"How about you, Debby?" Dad asks.

"I guess I'm partly ready."

"Great. Let's have our reports."

"Let me go first!" says Heather. She reaches under her chair and retrieves five books. "I went to the library and found some exciting books about New Orleans and Louisiana in general. It looks like a great place to visit. We won't be going during Mardi Gras, but maybe that's just as well—things would really be crowded and would probably cost more."

"Give us some examples of places we could visit," Mom says.

"Well, we should see the French Quarter, of course. They have some neat restaurants there. Some street jazz, too. They don't let cars onto Bourbon Street, so it's fun just to wander there on foot."

"During the daytime, that is," Dad pitches in, "Bourbon Street isn't a very good place for kids at night."

"There are lots of other things to do in these books," Heather responds. "There's a little ferry that would be fun to go on. There's the site where Andrew Jackson fought the Battle of New Orleans in the War of 1812. I'd love to check out short cruises on the Mississippi, or it might be fun to take a drive across the causeway that crosses Lake Pontchartrain. We can keep these books all week; how about letting everybody look through them and make a list of personal favorite ideas?"

"Let's do it," says Dad. "Jim, give us your report. You were going to find out about things we could see on the way."

"Well, there's a lot we can see between Dallas and New Orleans. If we want to drive through Houston we could take a tour of the NASA Space Center. We could go from there down to the Gulf to play in the surf for a while, and maybe look for some shells. Or, if we wanted to, we could skip Houston and drive through the Big Thicket. After we get into Louisiana, we could drive right along the coast and stop at the Jungle Gardens and Bird City just south of New Iberia."

"Good report, Jim," says Mom. "Let me look at your maps."

Dad turns to Debby. "You were going to make a list of games we could play along the way. What did you find, Debby?"

"Mommy got me a book to help me," she says. "But I didn't understand the rules very well."

"I'm sorry, honey," Mom says. "I'll sit down with you after school tomorrow and we'll read them together."

"We're making some good progress," Dad says. "This is going to be a great trip. After we look through the books, let's make a final decision on the places we want to visit, both in New Orleans and on the way. Then, Heather and Jim, I want you to write to those places and find out what their hours are and their costs. Okay?"

Assignments and Resources

The Rice family has given us a good example of how to go about the planning phase of the trip. We can spend some time around the dinner table discussing ideas and finding out what different family

□

members would like to do. Or we call a family meeting and formalize the process a little bit.

One caution: If the sky is <u>not</u> the limit, don't let your children think it is. You may wish to set some parameters on the trip from the very beginning. "We're going to take a trip to Washington, D.C., later this summer. Let's talk about what you'd like to do there." Or "Would you rather take a trip to Vancouver or to the Grand Canyon?"

After you've settled on your general destination, it's time to make some assignments. If you have children in fifth or sixth grade or older, they'll be able to do some simple library research. It's fun for them to get involved in making recommendations about what you can do on the trip. Older kids can also review the road atlas and material from auto clubs, or write to chambers of commerce and specific attractions.

The Rice family likes to assign one child to gather information on the destination and another child to get material on attractions along the way. But one mother of smaller children does all the research herself. Once she has built a nice collection of material (brochures, pamphlets, maps, pictures), she puts it all together into a scrapbook. Then she goes through the scrapbook with each of her kids.

No matter who makes your plan, remember that many children have a limited attention span. Plan a variety of activities for a given day, or plan a single activity that has built-in variety. Also, to avoid wearing everybody out—including yourself—avoid taking whirlwind tours. Instead, find a central location that you can call "home" during your trip, and plan day-trips from there. This saves on travel time, on packing and unpacking each day, and on the frustration of trying to find a new place to stay each night. It also gives the kids a certain amount of stability, which they will appreciate even on a trip.

After you've decided where you want to go on your trip, get out the maps and check distances from point to point so you can estimate how long each leg of the trip will last and where you will be each night.

A reminder: Even though it takes some time and planning to create a fantastic trip, no plan needs to be inflexible. If, after you get under way, you find no one's having fun, it's time to change your pace, or change the plan. Your goal isn't to fulfill the plan—it's to have a good time together.

Earning Your Way Together

How to get your kids to earn three hundred bucks, strictly for the family trip, by 3 p.m. Thursday.

The Kiholm family does yard work together, going out each Saturday for four or five hours to earn money for their trip.

The parents at the Robinsons' hire their kids to work around the house. The kids do everything from vacuuming, helping with the laundry, loading and unloading the dishwasher, and cleaning the toilets to mowing the lawn and washing the car.

The three older children at the Stouts' all have paying jobs. Two work at fast-food restaurants and one has a paper route. They all contribute a percentage of their earnings to the family fund, which is reserved for family trips. The two younger children, who receive allowances, also contribute a percentage.

All these families practice an important principle: When everyone earns and contributes, all family members have greater interest in and appreciation for a family vacation.

More Money-Making Tips

Older kids can usually earn money by getting a regular part-time job—working in a grocery store or a dime store, for instance. Younger children can do extra work around the house and get paid accordingly. But many children can also make money by being entrepreneurs, selling needed items or services in the neighborhood.

Here are some ideas on how your kids can earn money to help pay for the trip—or simply to spend on souvenirs for themselves:

• mowing lawns and doing other yard care

• selling garden seeds in the springtime

- selling garden produce in the fall
- helping to clean neighbors' homes and garages
- babysitting
- getting a newspaper route
- selling Christmas cards and Christmas wrapping paper
- shoveling snow from driveways and sidewalks
- collecting aluminum cans
- selling snack foods at parks and along parade routes
- delivering leaflets and handbills

These ideas are just to get you started. Libraries have books that are filled with ideas on how kids can make money.

Getting Prepared

How to do eighty hours of work before you leave on your trip in twenty hours, when you feel a cold coming on.

The more you prepare in advance, the less harried and frustrated you will be when it's time to leave on the trip.

And there's a lot to be said for less frustration!

While we'd all prefer to leave on vacation relaxed and

ready and <u>liking</u> each other, the reality for most of us is that the extra tasks of packing and planning and making arrangements for the house/mail/pets/ newspaper can leave us frazzled. If everybody's clothes for the trip are clean and packed in advance, what about clothes to wear in the <u>meantime</u>? Kids who will miss their friends would rather not spend their last days at home doing housework. Pressure to have everything under control at work before leaving may mean Dad's out of patience and time for mowing the lawn once more before departure. But it <u>is</u> possible to fit the extra work into odd moments and to keep everybody happy and enthusiastic. The secret is to acknowledge each person's needs and pitch in to help each other out. Once again, a little advance planning can make an enormous difference.

The first thing to do when you're trying to get ready for a trip is to make two lists: a list of everything you need to accomplish before you leave, and a list of everything you need to pack for the trip. For instance:

To Do Before We Leave

☐ 1. Get the car checked out: oil, lube, belts, hoses, tires, etc.

☐ 2. Go through the bills and make sure they're paid up till after we get home

☐ 3. Buy each of the kids a new outfit for the trip, just for fun

☐ 4. Make sure any prescriptions are up to date and full enough to last the trip

10

☐

☐ 5. Buy travelers' checks

☐ 6. Find someone to feed the dogs while we're gone

☐ 7. Get the Helprins to watch our house while we're gone; ask Bob if he'll take care of our trash

☐ 8. Have the post office hold our mail

☐ 9. Go shopping—pick up snacks and meals for the trip

☐ 10. Wash all the clothes we'll need to take

☐ 11. Choose one location in the house to "stockpile" whatever we're taking and organize things there

☐ 12. Have each family member list personal "take-alongs" and then discuss compromises that avoid duplication and save space

☐ 13. Check the timers we'll use on our lights and radio for home security purposes

☐ 14. Make reservations for the motel and so forth

□

To Take on the Trip

- [ ] 1. Three complete changes of clothes for everybody
- [ ] 2. Games
- [ ] 3. Blankets and pillows
- [ ] 4. Food and water
- [ ] 5. Toiletries for all
- [ ] 6. Whatever book I'm reading that week
- [ ] 7. and so forth.

A more complete list of things you may want to take follows in "Things to Take".

You may save some valuable time in the long run by making complete lists specifically for your family, photocopying them, and using them (with minor adaptations) time after time.

As you look at your lists, you may begin to feel overwhelmed. That's the time to consider delegating some of the tasks to others. You're going on the trip for the benefit and enjoyment of <u>everyone</u> in the family, so it's reasonable to expect that <u>everyone</u> can help in preparing to go on the trip.

Unfortunately, no matter how carefully you plan, you can't eliminate the chance for something to go wrong. But the more prepared you are, the less likely it is that some last-minute emergency will spoil your departure. Expect the unexpected, and be ready to enjoy.

HOT TIP—If you're planning to go to any museums or nice restaurants on your trip, and if your children are young, try this: Have them practice the desired behavior in your own home. As you eat dinner together say, "Tonight we're pretending to be eating in a restaurant. I'll help you know how you should behave."

After you've practiced a few times in your home, you may want to visit a <u>local</u> museum or restaurant to see how well they've learned.

Things to Take

How to sort through all the things your kids insist on taking on the trip: a stereo with maxi-speakers, nine pounds of books, a case of graham crackers, three changes of clothes for each day you'll be gone, twenty-three pairs of shoes, and a pet parakeet.

What should you take on the trip? The answer is not as obvious as it may seem. Many families have found themselves a hundred miles from home and tired without any pillows in the car. ("After all, we knew the motel was going to supply its own pillows.") On the other hand, too many families have struggled through a cross-country trip with so much stuff on the floor and stacked around the children that no one was able to move.

The secret, of course, is to find a happy medium. **Don't take things you won't need; don't leave behind things you will need.** This is another reason to make the master list mentioned in the previous section. And if you keep the list from trip to trip, you'll be able to refine it, adding items you may have forgotten earlier, and taking off things you've found you really don't need.

A Few Suggestions

Don't forget to take the following:

- [ ] A complete change of clothes for everybody— one for each day you'll be gone (unless you intend to stop sometime and use a laundromat)— plus

- [ ] Shoes and other equipment suited to special planned activities

- [ ] Toiletries—shampoo, deodorant, toothbrushes, toothpaste, shaving gear, perfume, sanitary napkins and/or tampons

- [ ] Blow dryers, hair curlers, brushes, combs, and so forth

- [ ] Cash, checkbook, credit cards, travelers' checks

- [ ] Blankets and pillows

- [ ] Food

- [ ] Water

- [ ] Vitamins

- [ ] Pre-moistened wipes for cleaning up messes (or a damp washcloth in a plastic bag) and paper towels

- [ ] Medicines, just in case—aspirin substitutes, cold medicines, cough medicines, something for upset stomach, something for motion sickness

☐ A basic first-aid kit
(include the medicines
just mentioned, plus
Band-Aids®, gauze
bandages, adhesive
tape, rubbing
alcohol, hydrogen
peroxide, your
favorite medicated
lotion for insect bites
and sunburn,
thermometer, scissors,
first aid instruction book)

☐ Games to play along the way and other things to
keep the kids occupied: paper and pencil,
coloring books, toys, and so forth (see Section 3,
"Fun on the Way," for other ideas)

☐ Baby supplies, if needed—food, bottles and
formula, at least two pacifiers (one will get lost—
count on it!), disposable diapers, plastic pants if
your baby's disposable diapers tend to leak, bibs,
and a stroller and/or backpack

☐ This book, for many helps along the way

Here are a few items you might not usually think of:

☐ Self-closing plastic bags to hold those treasures
your kids will find along the way

☐ A plastic ice cream bucket, with lid, for those
"bathroom" emergencies when the next rest
stop is ten miles down the road

- [ ] Toilet paper
- [ ] A plastic bag for wet and dirty clothes
- [ ] A travel alarm clock
- [ ] A can or bottle opener
- [ ] Nail clippers
- [ ] A small sewing kit
- [ ] A flashlight

A Few Clothing Tips

As you're thinking of what clothing to take, you'll want to keep a few basic ideas in mind.

- First, try to have things do double duty. For instance, take only one coat or jacket, even if you normally wear two in a given week at home. Take only one pair of shoes, if possible. (And definitely don't try to break in a new pair of shoes on a trip.)

- Second, take clothing that can be worn in several different combinations, giving yourself many outfits from just a few items.

- Third, take clothing that can be layered, which will help you adjust to changes in climate and weather.

- Fourth, take clothes that will require the least amount of care.

Tips for Packing

How to fit three cubic feet of clothing into a two-cubic-foot space.

Does it matter <u>how</u> you pack things for the trip? Ben Rigby tells this experience:

"In one of our recent trips the atmosphere in the car quickly degenerated into chaos. No, I'm not talking about the behavior of the children—though I wasn't totally satisfied with that either—but about the physical surroundings.

"We left in such a hurry that we didn't take time to think through how things were arranged in the luggage or in the car. Ordinarily, everything has a place and there's a place for everything. Unfortunately, we overlooked that this time.

"We had been gone only twenty minutes when the baby needed to be changed. Trish rummaged around in the bags until she found a diaper, right on the bottom of the clothes bag. She emptied out the top layers and pulled out the diaper, then turned to the task of changing.

"While she was busy doing that, our two boys got into the food. We yelled at them, but we were a little slow, and some of the damage had already been done.

"After the baby was changed, Trish became preoccupied with reconstructing the food bag while I was busy driving in heavy traffic. Our boys started to explore the other bags Trish had packed and stuck at random in the back seat. They pulled out an assortment of clothes and armfuls of toys and had a grand time, quietly, until we caught them.

"That's when things really started to get bad. . . ."

Does it matter how you pack? The question answers itself.

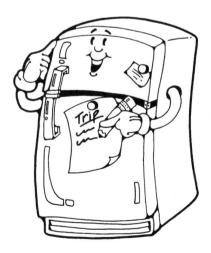

The starting point is to make a master list of everything to take. As we mentioned in an earlier section, it can be very helpful to make a list that you use over and over again, refining and improving it as time passes. You may want to hang the list on the refrigerator or some other prominent place, or reproduce it and give copies to everyone in the family who is going to help in the packing. Be sure to mark those copies so each person knows what his or her tasks are.

Who Should Do the Packing?

Packing chores can probably be divided according to the age of the children involved: Older children (say, ages nine and up) can pack their own things from the master list; middle children (ages six through eight) can collect their own things for Mom's or Dad's inspection before packing; smaller children (five and under) will be of little help in packing; Mom or Dad should pack for them.

What Is the Best Way to Pack?

Everything-in-suitcases is not necesarily the best way to pack. Here is an assortment of methods, all used by experienced families to meet their individual needs:

□

- Pack nice clothes—dressy clothes—in one suitcase. Then everything will be together for your "dressed-up" event and you'll be able to protect those clothes better.

- Pack all pajamas, toothbrushes, and other bedtime gear together in one suitcase.

- Let each child have his or her own small gym bag or backpack or duffel bag.

- Put extra shoes together in one bag.

- Pack together all the outfits for one day.

- Roll outfits together. Rolling saves space and enables you to keep things together better.

- If you don't want to roll your clothes, some travelers lay clothing flat rather than fold it.

- Put together everything for one day. Thus, you might have a bag for Wednesday, which contains all the clothing for every member of the family, another bag for Thursday, and so forth. Then you have to load and unload only one bag each night, not many.

- Use plastic garbage bags instead of suitcases. They fit better in odd spaces and take up exactly as much space as their contents, but no more.

- Take a separate bag for dirty clothes and a plastic bag for wet clothing.

- Pack all swimming things in one small bag, along with a brush or comb.

□

- Pack nightclothes on top so they're easy to get out at night.

- Before packing, transfer all liquids (including perfumes and prescription drugs) to plastic bottles.

- Use self-closing plastic bags to hold toothbrushes, shower items, medicines, hair-care items, jewelry, and so forth.

- Use plastic holders with tight-fitting lids for hair-care items and makeup.

- Let your kids bring a small bag of things to do on the way, using a small tote bag, a drawstring denim bag, a gym bag, or whatever suits your situation. (One family has their children pack this bag only half full, so there's space for souvenirs and "treasures" obtained along the way.)

Choose the combination of packing methods best suited for your family. For example, teenagers may resist having their clothing lumped in with everyone else's, but they can understand (and even be in charge of!) putting all the fishing gear or everybody's hiking boots together in one bag.

Remember as you pack that everything has to come back out of those bags while you're on the way. Plan so that your four-year-old won't have to dig past your only tie and dress shirt to find her sneakers.

On longer trips or if there's a mishap of some kind, you may need to stop to wash your clothes at a laundromat. Don't try to keep children occupied at the laundromat while the clothes are rinsing and spinning. Instead, have one parent sit at the laundromat with a book or magazine while the other takes the kids to the park or a movie.

What Is a Good Way to Arrange Things in the Car?

Remember that where you pack things can make a big difference in how well your trip goes. Leave easy access to food and water. Keep diapers handy. Have available a change of clothes for little ones who might have an accident of some kind or other. Place games and other activity items where you can reach them. While you will want all these things handy for you, you may want to arrange them so young children cannot reach them. Otherwise, turn your head for just a moment and suddenly you're in the middle of a big mess.

□

As you load the car, just as when you're packing your bags, keep in mind the frequency and order in which you're likely to need different things. Don't be afraid to be creative about where and how you put things: if it <u>works</u>, it's <u>right</u>!

One final tip: As you travel about, count your bags and suitcases just as you count your children. More than one family has saved much trouble and headache by taking a quick inventory each time they load or unload.

Preparing Your Home

How to let neighbors know you're gone and make burglars think you're home.

The Steadmans once made a last-minute decision to go on a vacation. They quickly threw together some clothes, climbed into the car, and took off.

They didn't bother to tell any of the neighbors that they were leaving.

And they left the house a disaster site. Jill Steadman, the mother in the family, wasn't overly excited about returning to a dirty house, but what choice did she have?

The Steadmans traveled across Texas and into New Mexico. They had never visited Carlsbad Caverns, but thought that would be a great destination. They were having a wonderful time.

Meanwhile, their next-door neighbor began to get a little worried. She hadn't seen any of the Steadmans for several days. Their garage door was closed and locked, so she couldn't tell if their cars were there. Ordinarily, she saw Alan Steadman go off to work every day, and she saw the kids walk up the street to catch the bus. Rarely did many days go by without a good talk with Jill.

What if something had happened to them?

She walked over and rang the doorbell. No answer. She pounded on the door. No answer. She peered through the window. The place was in total disarray, apparently ransacked.

Where was the family? Her imagination ran wild. Had they been murdered? Her heart throbbed in her throat. She ran back home and called the police. They came, peered through the window, and agreed. Some violent crime had happened in the Steadman home.

They broke in the door.

But no one was there.

The Steadmans drove up while the police were still in their home. They saw three police cars parked in front of their house. They saw the front door hanging open. What could have happened while they were gone?

Eventually everything was all sorted out. But only after great embarrassment to Alan and Jill Steadman.

Arlen Chidester was a little wiser. He took the time to tell a trusted neighbor he was leaving, and he gave

her a key to his house so she could water his plants. On the third day she entered the home to tend to the plants and discovered that Arlen's water heater had rusted out and was pouring water all over the basement floor. Some damage had already occurred, but she was able to turn off the water and prevent further damage.

These two stories illustrate extremes, but you need not have such experiences to realize how beneficial it can be to let a trusted neighbor know when you leave town.

Cleanliness, Economy, and Security

Few experiences are more discouraging than returning home tired and relaxed only to be confronted with clutter and chaos. While "deep cleaning" is probably too much to expect in the midst of getting ready for a trip, anything you can do to tidy up as you go will be a relief and a pleasure to you when you get back.

At the very least, make sure that food has been cleaned from the garbage disposal and clean out the refrigerator. Give perishable food to a friend or neighbor. Make sure all the toilets have been flushed– then check again as all the children are going out the door for the last time.

Your next two concerns should be economy and security. What can you do to save money on the house while you're not using it? What should you do to make sure the house is safe while you're not around? Use the following checklist to help you get your house ready.

Checklist for Preparing Your House

☐ Eliminate clutter throughout

☐ Clean out refrigerator—perishables

☐ Run garbage disposal

☐ Flush toilets—double check!

☐ Take out garbage

☐ Close fireplace flue

☐ Turn down water heater and furnace

☐ Unplug televisions, radios, computers, electric blankets, and so forth

☐

☐ Make sure water faucets are turned off tightly

☐ If you're going to be gone a month or more, contact the phone company and ask if they have a vacation rate (Sometimes if a customer is going to be gone for an extended period of time, the phone company will charge them only half or less.)

☐ Set some of the lights and a radio on a timer, so it appears that someone is home

☐ Notify the post office not to deliver mail, and

☐ Have newspaper delivery stopped while you're gone, or

☐ Have a neighbor pick up all your mail and newspapers

☐ Ask a neighbor to watch your house

☐ Water your plants thoroughly; if you'll be gone over a week, see if a neighbor will check on them

☐ Take your pets to a kennel or arrange for a friend to take care of them

☐ Hire someone to water and mow your lawn

☐ Hire a student to shovel snow from your driveway and sidewalk while you're gone

☐ If necessary, ask a neighbor to take your garbage cans out to the street and return the empties to their place

☐ Lock and bolt all doors and windows

☐ Close all your drapes and curtains

☐ Lock your garage door

☐ Remove valuables from your house and put them in a safe deposit box—money, jewelry, bonds, and so forth

☐ Leave a list of the serial numbers of your travelers' checks with a trusted friend, in case you lose both your checks and your own separate list of numbers

☐ Don't broadcast news of your departure to strangers—they may take the opportunity to burglarize your home in your absence

☐ Leave a copy of your trip itinerary with a friend or neighbor, including phone numbers (if possible), so you can be contacted in an emergency. Do the same with a family member, in case there is a family emergency.

Comfort on the Way

$$\triangledown$$

Comfort on the Way

Comfort in the Car

How to travel nonstop for a thousand miles in a Honda Civic, and get your children to sleep the entire way.

You can enjoy a trip with your children much more if you give some thought to keeping them **comfortable** and **entertained** en route. When you're traveling by car, this can be a constant challenge.

Tips for car comfort:

Limit the number of hours you drive each day.

Even adults get tired after hours upon hours of steady driving. It seems to be even harder for kids. To keep everybody happier, try to limit your driving each day to only five or six hours. Plan ahead; choose your destination for the end of the day, and wind up your driving before everyone is totally exhausted and wondering what's so fun about family trips.

If you do plan ahead, you can often arrive at your destination for the day well before bedtime. That's when your kids will really start to enjoy the trip. Drive for a few hours, then stop and enjoy yourselves—go for a swim, take in a movie, visit the park, see the sights in the city or town where you're staying.

And don't forget to make some sightseeing or entertainment stops along the way.

If you really must have some days of long, long driving as part of your trip, try to break them up. Perhaps you can have a long drive every other day, with a short drive and more relaxation in between.

Be wise in your use of space in the car.

The ideal situation is to have a car big enough to accommodate all the family at once. Room for every person to have his or her own seat is basic; even better would be to have some extra room, room for each person to move around a bit, room for some to lie down if they wish.

One of the most enjoyable trips one family ever took was in a rented motor home. They had four children at the time, and the motor home had room to sleep exactly six. As they traveled, the children had plenty of room to sleep, to lounge and read, to play games together, to stretch their legs. The kids still talk about that trip—and wonder when the family is going to do it again.

Even if you don't have the luxury of traveling in a home on the road, even if your car doesn't have a lot of room, you can try to set things up so you're using your space wisely.

If your car doesn't have enough room for both family and luggage, and if there isn't room in the trunk, put the luggage on a rack on the roof. Be sure to secure it tightly!

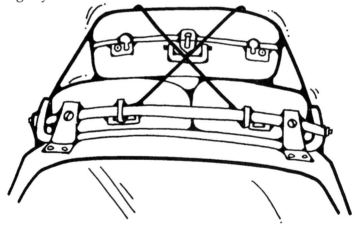

Part of the wise use of space involves putting your children in the right places in the car. Some families give each child his own space. He can put his stuff there and call it his own. Others have more success in having the children rotate through the car every hour or every hundred miles, giving each one a turn at each spot. This will allow each child a chance to sit by the window and a chance to sit by Mom and Dad.

For some families, even these suggestions don't eliminate all the friction. If you find yourself in this situation, don't lose hope. Read the next idea.

Travel when your kids will sleep.

One family has five children and a car that will seat six people comfortably. When they travel, the cramped conditions in the car quickly lead to discomfort, which then grows into bickering kids and frustrated parents. Their solution: "We always travel at night. Then it's quiet and peaceful and nice."

Other families use variations on this idea. One family starts their trip in the wee hours of the morning, when the parents have had some rest and can drive more safely, but the children are still tired and will fall back asleep. Another plans their driving time to coincide with the children's nap times.

Even in a crowded car, the kids can sleep. At night, they will likely fall asleep every which way, finding a (relatively) comfortable position in the same way that water fills in gaps. During the daytime, have them take turns sleeping on each other's laps. Whether they're going to be sleeping or not, you may want to take a couple of blankets and pillows.

Find ways to increase comfort in the car itself.

One of great curses of traveling in the summer without air conditioning in the car is the horrible noise that comes in through the windows. The Niemans have made many trips in a van that doesn't have air conditioning. When they crank the windows down, the road noise and wind noise grow so loud that they literally have to shout to communicate with one another. Those are not exactly ideal conditions for a nice family trip.

If you don't have air conditioning and can't afford to buy a new car just to get it, there are a few things you can do to increase comfort a little. Buy a small auto fan (available at an auto-parts store), and install it on your

dashboard. Or hang special auto shades over the windows to cut down the glare and to provide some shade. These are designed not to obstruct the vision of the driver. Finally, provide sunglasses for everyone in the car.

In the winter, make sure your heater works. Nothing is worse than driving from the warm south up into the cold north only to discover that your heater is broken. The Lewises did exactly that—but only once. That was enough to teach them a lesson.

Wear comfortable clothing.

Your children will be much more comfortable in general if they're wearing the right clothing. Loose clothing is best. Tight clothes restrict circulation, which results in subtle discomfort. It is also helpful to layer the clothing your children wear. When they get warm, they can take off layers. When they get too cold, they can add layers.

Make frequent rest stops.

Remember that the trip—not the destination—is
your goal.

Experienced travelers agree that it's more important to
give the family an occasional rest—even though that
causes delay—than to push quickly on toward the day's
destination. The constant motion and confinement in the
car tend to have a wearing effect that accumulates as the
hours pass. The only way to provide a positive release is
to stop the car and let the kids out. A little rest can go a
long way.

There are a number of effective ways to utilize rest stops:

• Stop where everybody can use the restroom.

• Stop at a schoolground or park to play or picnic.

• Let the children play for a
few minutes at every
stop—they can toss a ball,
throw a frisbee, jump
rope, or just run. One
father picks out a nearby
landmark and has his
children run out to it and
back.

• Stop on a regular basis—
every fifty or one hundred
miles, or every hour
or two.

• Let the children know
when the next stop is
coming—"We'll stop

promptly at 3 o'clock." Or, "We'll stop when the odometer reads 61,300." Or, "We'll stop at the very next highway rest stop."

- Limit each stop to ten or fifteen minutes—but let the children know that when it's time to stop to eat, you'll stop for a whole hour.

- Sometimes it's nice to stop at a convenience store and let the kids go in with you to buy a treat.

Safety in the Car

How to make the round trip without accident or injury.

Manny Tyler was getting tired. He'd been driving for three hours without stopping, and his eyelids were beginning to droop. His wife and three children slept, their quiet breathing filling his ears. Their sleep seemed to be catching. He yawned and rubbed his eyes.

$\triangledown$

The road rolled under his wheels in a steady rhythm. *I'd better stop,* he thought. *Maybe I should pull over and let Lydia drive.* He almost did, but then decided not to. If he stopped the car, everyone would likely wake up. Then they'd be stirring and talking and he wouldn't be able to sleep anyway.

No, he'd continue. He could sleep later.

His head began to nod. He opened the wing window and let the breeze blow on his face. *Got to wake up,* he thought. *I don't know how much longer I can take this.*

The next thing he knew, the car was speeding across the shoulder and down an embankment. He tried to get control of the car, but it was too late . . .

Nothing is more important on a trip than the safety of the travelers.

Reaching a destination on time may be desirable, and comfort considerations are necessary—but <u>nothing</u> is more important than safety.

Here are a few rules of safety to keep in mind:

<u>Rule 1</u>: Never drive when you are too tired. Trade with another driver, or pull off to the side of the road and rest.

<u>Rule 2</u>: Make frequent rest stops. This is as important for the driver as it is for passengers. A short break will increase circulation, clear the head, provide a change of pace.

Rule 3: All passengers in the car must wear seatbelts.

Rule 4: Babies must remain in carseats at all times.

Rule 5: Children must not touch any controls on the dashboard or steering column.

Rule 6: The driver may not carry a child on his or her lap. (Obeying Rule 3 will eliminate problems here.)

Rule 7: Children may not play with sharp or hard objects in the car. Toys should be soft; crayons are safer than pencils.

Rule 8: Children may not be too noisy. That distracts the driver and is unsafe.

Rule 9: Children may not hang hands or feet or other objects out of the windows.

Rule 10: Passengers using headphones must keep the volume low. Loud music or loud talk through headphones can damage the ears, and if everyone's listening to something different, the driver is as isolated as if he were all alone.

Seatbelts Are Proven Life Savers

It's appropriate to say a bit more about Rule 3, since wearing seatbelts is one of the most important—and most violated—of all the rules of safety. In many jurisdictions, the law now requires all drivers and passengers to use seatbelts.

Studies show that more children die in automobile crashes than from any single disease. Thousands are killed or injured every year. Usually the injury is caused by the impact of being thrown against the dashboard, the back of the seat, or into or through the window. Seatbelts have been proven over and over again to significantly diminish the risk of injury in the case of an accident.

In fact, when passengers are wearing seatbelts, *fatal* or *serious* injuries are reduced by 40–50 percent.

(U. S. Department of Transportation, National Center for Statistics and Analysis)

Some parents agree with wearing seatbelts in theory, but they're unsure how to get their children to do it. "It's just not worth the hassle," they say. "I'd rather just drive safely than put up with the trouble of fighting with kids over their seatbelts." But driving safely is not a fail-proof way to avoid accidents, and death or serious injury cannot be reversed.

How can we get our kids to wear their seatbelts? Here are a few suggestions from a variety of parents:

- Set the example by always wearing your own seatbelt. Explain that wearing your own seatbelt is something everybody does, even Mommy and Daddy.

- Start kids with seatbelts from the very beginning. Make sure they know that that's always a part of riding in a car.

- Never go any where without seatbelts on. If you always wear them on short trips–even to the grocery store–the kids will expect to wear them on longer trips.

- Make sure your child can see out the window with the seatbelt on. You may need to buy a special seat for him or her to sit on.

- Before leaving, always check to see if everyone has a seatbelt on. Check periodically during the trip to make sure no one has taken it off. If someone does, pull over and stop the car until he puts it back on.

- Remember to praise children each time they put on their seatbelts without being reminded.

- Allow your kids to listen to tapes or play games only when they have their seatbelts on. If they take the seatbelt off, take the tape or game away until they comply.

- Make it a rule that if seatbelts aren't buckled up, the car doesn't get turned on. One family makes a game of seeing who can buckle up first: starting with all family members seated with hands up, on the count of 3 (2 for the very smallest child), everybody races.

Whatever approach you decide to try, don't give in. Persistence is vital. Don't let the children get away with violating the seatbelt rule. Their lives are too important for that.

Your Own Rules for the Road

*How to get normal children to behave like angels
in a car with no room to run, no bathrooms, no TV,
and no phone.*

What kind of rules should you have for the road? The
objectives are happiness and quiet. Discipline is not
the kind of activity the family looks forward to on the
annual vacation, but making and enforcing
meaningful rules for the trip is essential. It will help
everyone understand and agree on limits, and that will
increase safety and unity in the car.

Different families have different rules: "No spitwads in
the car." "Put on your headphones and don't bother
anybody." "No asking how long till we get there."
"The driver gets to pick the music." "A McDonald's
order may not exceed $40."

Others are perhaps a little more significant: "Whenever
we get into the car, each person is to call out an
assigned letter in our last name, in order, so we know
everyone is present." "No littering of any kind. Use
the trash bag we bring along." "No fighting. If
someone gets crabby and starts bickering, he has to sit
with his hand over his mouth for ten minutes. If he
hits, he has to hold his hands up in the air." "No going
to the restroom alone. And whenever we stop at the
rest stop, everyone has to go."

Three Keys to a Peaceful Trip

Of course, making rules is different from enforcing
them. But the way you enforce rules when traveling is
the same as the way you enforce them at home. If you

have control of your children at home, then you'll find it much easier to control them on a trip.

Because a car is a different environment than a home, you may want a few strategies in addition to those you use at home.

Here are three keys to help you keep your kids quiet and happy on the road:

1. Make sure they are as comfortable as possible (see Section II A).

2. Make sure they are occupied and entertained (you'll find dozens of great ideas in Section III).

3. Set simple, enforceable rules to encourage them to make good choices.

Food on the Way

How your family can have their own fast food operation on wheels.

The Erdmanns were only an hour into their trip when little Jed began to whine. "I want a drink of water," he said, his voice high and unpleasant. "I'm thirsty."
"I'm sorry, honey," his mom said. "We forgot to bring a jug of water."

"But I'm thirsty," he whined. "I want a drink of water right now!"

The Liljenquists had been traveling for an hour and a half. Mom opened their small cooler. "Time for lunch, kids," she announced.

44

"I'm starved," Dorrie said. "What are we having?"

Mom pulled out a stack of sandwiches wrapped in baggies. "Tuna fish sandwiches, with pickles in them." She rummaged in the cooler. "And some bananas."

The smell of tuna and pickle and overripe banana filled the small car.

Dorrie wrinkled her nose and sat back in her seat. "Maybe I'll eat later," she said. "My tummy's not feeling too good."

_____

The Hoaglands had been traveling for a hour when the mom, Margie, opened the small cooler she'd brought. "Who wants a snack?" she asked.

"I do!" the kids said, almost in unison.

"I thought you might." She passed out little containers of finger gelatin she had prepared before leaving. She handed each child a granola bar, then gave them all drinks.

Two hours later the dad pulled into a town to get some gas. "It's about time for dinner," he said. "I thought we'd buy a hamburger somewhere. Anybody have an appetite yet?"

"I do!" the kids chorused.

Eating on a trip is one way to keep mouths quiet, hands busy, and faces happy. Of course, we need to remember to take what's needed—rather than things that will tend to cause our children to lose their appetites.

We can learn from the mistakes of the Erdmanns and the Liljenquists, and follow the good example of the Hoaglands.

Tips on Traveling with Food

<u>Preparing Before You Go</u>

- Create menus for the meals you'll be preparing on the way.

- Consider delegating responsibility for meals, with a different person in charge of each.

- Get a cooler to store food and drink.

- Purchase plenty of paper cups, paper towels, and pre–moistened towelettes (or wet washcloths in self-closing plastic bags).

- Get a lap-sized cutting board for preparing sandwiches and cutting fruit.

- Make a list of all the things you'll need—food and food-preparation items—and collect them in one place.

- Consider getting an individual non-spill cup for each member of the family. Some manufacturers make kiddie cups with sipping lids that cut down on spills.

- Remember to consider the likes and dislikes of family members. The confinement of traveling by car can make fussy appetites worse and exaggerate strong odors of certain foods.

- Get a couple of old sheets to place over the car seats to protect them from food. You may wish to leave the sheets in place throughout the entire trip.

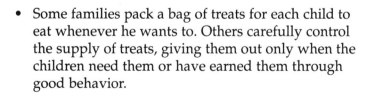

- Consider taking self-contained items: apples or bananas, little containers of juice, granola bars.

- Some families pack a bag of treats for each child to eat whenever he wants to. Others carefully control the supply of treats, giving them out only when the children need them or have earned them through good behavior.

- Pack a lunch for the first day so it's all ready to eat.

Hints for Meals

- You might want to cook a ham or turkey beforehand, and take the sliced meat along with rolls, with the condiments and dressings already on the rolls.

- Sandwiches are old standbys: easy to fix on the way, relatively non-messy, and quite inexpensive.

- For breakfast, try buying paper bowls, plastic spoons, a carton of milk, a box or two of cold cereal, and some fruit.

- Whether you fix your own sandwiches or buy them, mealtime is a good time to let the children run and play for a few minutes. Parks are great places for meals—your kids don't have to be nearly as quiet and neat as you would require them to be in a restaurant or in the car.

- Remember that a trip can be upsetting to a child's (or an adult's) digestive system. Feed your family on a regular schedule—not just snacks, but a real meal.

Be Creative with Food

- If you have a toddler, tie a bagel to his carseat to nibble on. When he gets hungry or bored it will be handy, and if he drops it, it won't fall to the floor.

- Give your children O-shaped cereal to string on shoe-string licorice or on yarn. When their creations are complete, they'll have a ready-made snack.

- Give your children stick pretzels and colored marshmallows and have them make figures to eat.

- One mother cuts an X in the end of the nipple of her baby's bottle and lets her "drink" strained baby food mixed with formula. (This kind of nipple is also available in many stores.)

Some General Cautions

- Keep the food cooler or box or bag close to a parent or older child so it will be handy when it's time to pass out the food and out of small children's reach at other times.

- Sticky foods will create a mess that will stay in the car for the rest of the trip.

- Sweet drinks will make the children thirstier in the long run.

- Sugar and caffeine may tend to make your children hyper. If so, avoid them. Caffeine is found in cola drinks and chocolate, as well as coffee and tea.

- Salty foods may be more trouble than they're worth, even though they're temporarily satisfying. They'll cause your children to drink more and will lead to more bathroom stops.

- Foods with strong smells may lead to car sickness.

A Potpourri of Foods to Take

What kinds of food do parents like to take on trips? Experienced travelers agree that the best idea is to choose foods your kids will like, foods that don't take too much room, foods that aren't too messy.

<u>**Fruit and vegetable groups**</u>
raisins
melons cut into cubes
apples
grapes
oranges
plums
bananas
carrot and celery sticks
olives
dried fruit
fruit rolls
individual baby jars filled with fruit— even big kids like them

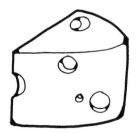

<u>**Breads and grains**</u>
granola bars
trail mix
crackers (with "squeeze cheese," if desired)
chips

rolls (can heat in the window)
banana bread, zucchini bread, etc.
popcorn (go easy on the salt)
regular wheat or white breads
sunflower seeds
teething biscuits for baby
corn nuts

Proteins
jerky
cheese slices, cheese cubes, or string cheese
yogurt
nuts
peanut butter (for sandwiches or celery)
boiled eggs
thin-sliced sandwich meats

Sweets

hard candies
lollipops
licorice
cookies
ice cream (if you have a motor home)
caramel corn
finger gelatin (not too sweet but
good finger food)
individual containers of pudding

Drinks
soft drinks
drink mixes
juices
mineral water with fruit juice
water—don't forget a full jug!

Car Sickness and Sickness on the Way

How to establish your own instant mobile dispensary.

Picture this, if you have the heart: You're in the middle of a wonderful trip. You're making good time down the freeway; everyone in the family is getting along; everyone seems to be in good spirits. Suddenly, you feel a tap on your shoulder.

"Mom, I think I'm going to throw up."

"Are you sure, honey?" you ask.

"Mmm-ummm," your little boy says, his face a sickly white.

"Sounds bad," your husband says. "I'd better pull over."

But he doesn't make it in time.

A little car sickness can go a long way toward taking the pleasure out of an otherwise wonderful trip.

The incidence of car sickness is probably much less now than it was twenty or thirty years ago. Now most of us are able to travel on smooth, straight freeways rather than on winding, bumpy roads. But almost every family gets to face the problems of car sickness at one time or another. Like the common cold, car sickness will probably be with us for many years to come.

Car sickness is caused by one or more of the following: the feeling of confinement, the feeling of motion, uncomfortable heat, food that doesn't agree. When two or more of these combine to create the problem, the feeling of sickness intensifies.

Car Sickness—Some Solutions

Luckily, car sickness isn't something that we simply have to live with. There <u>are</u> some steps we can take to deal with it.

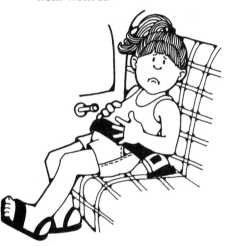

To start with, before you leave on your trip eat light, bland meals. Heavy food or spicy food can lead to nausea after you get under way. So can no food at all. Some mothers are careful to avoid milk—as it sits in the stomach it can lead to feelings of sickness.

Car sickness can be avoided in some children by making sure they don't get too hot and they do have plenty of fresh air. Air conditioning in the car usually helps. If you don't have air conditioning, you might need to let the sick child sit by the window with the air blowing in his face.

Don't let those who are prone to sickness read in the car. That intensifies the feelings of motion and of being closed in. Even those who are normally unaffected might begin to feel sick if they read in alternating sun and shadow.

If your child begins to feel sick, try having him sit in the front seat so he can see straight ahead. If necessary, elevate him so he can see through the windshield. It sometimes works to put a wet cloth on his forehead, hold a cold magazine against his tummy (this can be kept in your cooler), or have him chew gum.
You can also have some soothing drinks available: lemon-lime soft drinks, ginger ale, or a flat cola drink.

Try to distract your child. Read to him, play music, play games. Feed him saltine crackers. If you can, get him to take a nap.

Through all this, avoid talking about car sickness. Don't assume that your children will get car sick; assume that they won't, and take a positive attitude. Sometimes children begin to feel sick because someone put the idea into their heads. Try to avoid the whole issue, and they may not even think of getting sick.

If you've tried all the above and nothing works, you may need to use a motion-sickness drug. All medicines should be used only when absolutely necessary, and this is no exception. It tends to make some children drowsy or irritable or both. One dose of the typical over-the-counter motion-sickness drug is good for half a day. You should consult your doctor before giving it to your child.

Finally, the time may well come when one of your children throws up in the car. You can prepare for the event by bringing a paper lunch bag lined with a plastic bag. Keep it handy. If your child starts complaining about nausea, give him the bag and tell him to use it if necessary.

With car sickness, prevention is much better than cure. If one child should throw up in the car, even in a bag, others will begin to feel queasy. Just like the common cold, car sickness can be contagious!

Dealing with Other Sickness

Whether you have one child or many, your chances of someone's getting sick on a trip are fair—at least sooner or later. What can you do?

- Make sure your children are up to date on their physical checkups.

- Try to keep everyone in a regular routine for at least a couple of weeks preceding the trip. If your family is eating well and getting enough sleep you'll have a much better chance of everyone's staying healthy.

- Try to keep yourself and your children away from people who have communicable diseases, both before and on the trip.

- If your child is beginning to get sick as your departure date nears, you may need to postpone your trip a day or two or more. It may be inconvenient to change plans, but it will be worse than inconvenient to travel with a sick child.

- Take a small medicine bag with you on the trip, including medication to help with the ailments your children commonly get. Pack in the bag such things as cold medicine, aspirin substitute, cough medicine, something for upset stomach, something for diarrhea, something for sunburn (plus sunscreen, to help in prevention), and so forth. It is also a good idea to take along such medical staples as Band-Aids® and disinfectant.

3

Fun on the Way

Fun on the Way

Choosing and Carrying Playthings

How to turn the dullest stretch of road into a drive through Funland—at no extra cost!

What makes the difference between a fun trip and a boring, stressful one? A key difference comes from planning to make the travel itself fun.

A car certainly isn't a playland. But having fun in the car while you're traveling is the best way to make the time pass—and to make the trip truly memorable.

As you make plans for your trip, here are four essential ideas to keep in mind:

1. **Providing fun things for your children to do while traveling can improve everybody's mood—on the road and when you reach your destination.**

2. **The more you provide for a variety of fun activities, the more you'll be able to occupy your children for a long period of time.**

3. Surprise is one of the keys to fun on the trip. Keep the kids guessing what you'll give them to do next.

4. Good timing is critical. Plan two or three activities per hour, alternating one type of activity with a different type. If your kids want to stick with one activity, it's easy to let them, but be aware of short attention spans.

Activity Holders for Fun

One thing your children will really enjoy is to be able to use an "activity holder" for fun while they're traveling in the car. This will require some advance planning on your part, but it can be well worth it.

A number of different kinds of holders have been successfully used by different families. Some are simply variations of the others. Here are some approaches you'll want to consider:

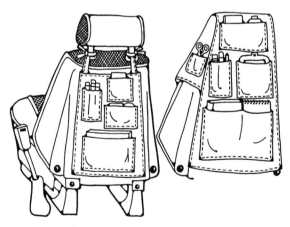

- Make a pocket apron or "car caddie" to hang over the back of the front seat, so the children in the back seat can use it. If you have room, you can make a different caddie for each child in your family. Fill the caddie's pockets with games and activities.

- Give each child a backpack with fun things in it.

- Let each child pack his own tote bag or backpack with fun things he wants access to on the road.

- Make "surprise boxes" for your children to use on the way. Inside the boxes can be such items as paper, tape, paper clips, scissors, markers, and so forth.

- Make a boredom grab bag by wrapping several fun toys and activity items. Mark each package with a number. Periodically (perhaps every two hours or one hundred miles), let your child pull a number from a sack. He can then play with the toy with that number.

- Wrap several little prizes. Mark on the outside of each package the name of a town you'll be passing along the way. When you pass the town, your child gets to open the prize. (If you won't be passing that many towns along the way, you can let your child unwrap the packages at certain mileage points.)

- Prepare a shoe box with small, inexpensive items inside it. Attach a string to each item, then hang the string outside the box and put the lid on. Every hour let each child pull one of the strings and have the item that's attached.

(If a child wants a toy or activity that someone selected earlier, he gets to have it after the hour is up, and the other child gets to pull a new string.)

- Give each child a metal cake pan with a lid on it. He can hold his activities inside the pan and use the surface for writing or coloring or playing.

- Organize the supplies for your in-car activities by putting each one in a separate self-closing plastic bag. Put all the bags together in one duffel bag or box. Hand them out one at a time, and require that the children hand their current item back before they get another one.

Here are some ideas for fun things you can include in your holders:

small books

a five-color ballpoint pen

magazines

pen and paper games

a small flannel board with flannel-backed pictures

magnets or magnetic letters in a metal can

prizes from cold cereal boxes

coins to spend along the way

postcards to write on .

The next section, "Toys and Supplies that Travel Well," contains a list of toys and games that you can also consider for holders.

Toys and Supplies that Travel Well

How to decide which toys to leave behind: the cap guns? the squirt guns? the box of Legos? the thousand-piece jigsaw puzzle? the doll stroller? the teddy bear family?

Your children no doubt have favorite things they will want to take along on your trip. Before you leave, talk with the kids about what to take and what to leave home. If possible, let them make some choices themselves. For example, a sleep-toy may be essential, but more than one may take up too much room. Letting a child select his own traveling companion can cut down on trauma at bedtime.

Here are two additional keys to keep in mind:

1. Remember that you'll be in a small space. Choose toys that don't require much room. Also choose toys that don't make much noise or mess.

○

2. Choose toys that aren't dangerous. When you're in a small enclosure, such as a car, toys that are quite safe in the home can become a problem. And those problems are magnified if you have to stop suddenly or if you have an accident.

Some Toys to Take

You know what's in your own toy box and game closet, and you know what is best for your children. But here are a few toys and ready-made games to consider:

Velcro® checkers

magnetic travel games (chess, checkers, backgammon)

card games

trivia games

electronic games

coloring books

crayons (brand new ones are great for trips, but keep them out of the hot sun!)

markers

activity books

sticker books

mazes (after kids solve them, they can color them in geometric patterns)

dolls and doll clothes

plastic play figures—cowboys, dinosaurs, farm animals, etc.

stroller attachment toys

magic slates

finger puppets

a small chalkboard with chalk and eraser

miniature cars

crossword puzzles

nesting toys

puppets

nontoxic molding clay

straws and soft pipe cleaners

sewing cards and yarn

A Few Activities

In a few pages we'll be giving you ideas about dozens of games you can play as you travel. But first, here are several activities you may want to have your children do in addition to games:

A scrapbook

Give each child an empty scrapbook at the beginning of the trip. As you travel, they can keep track of sites visited, places stayed, meals eaten, and so forth. Their scrapbooks can include pamphlets, brochures, maps, postcards, guides, drawings,

matchbook covers, soap wrappers from the hotel, nature objects, and anything else you or the child can think of.

A journal
Give each child an empty notebook or journal at the beginning of the trip. Encourage each to write details of the trip each day. They can describe the landscape you pass through, talk about what family members do and say as they travel, write about their favorite parts of the trip, record their feelings, and so on.

Teach macrame
Collect all the necessary supplies before you leave on your trip, then teach your children how to do macrame on the way. (Some have recommended doing knitting or crocheting in the car, but we would discourage this—the needles can be dangerous in a moving vehicle.)

Homemade tapes
Before you leave on your trip, Mom or Dad or both can fill cassette tapes with stories, songs, jokes, and riddles. Then let the kids listen to the tapes on the way. (One family ends their homemade tape with a "secret message" to the children, telling them where in the car a treat is hidden.)

Send postcards
Have your children write and send postcards to friends at home. Equally fun, have them send postcards to themselves, to read when they get home. Parents can also secretly send cards home to the kids to read when they get home.

Travel beads
Before you leave, prepare a string with beads for each child. Every twenty-five or fifty miles, let the child

remove a bead. If you can, plan it so that your child will remove the last bead precisely when you reach your destination.

Sorting games
Before you leave, gather a batch of small items for your preschooler to sort—buttons, cards, coins, dried beans, shells, corks, and so forth. Mix them all together and let your child sort them into muffin tins or the styrofoam boxes that hamburgers or eggs come in. (Caution: If your car is crowded, all the items might spill. And, of course, you won't want to give this activity to a child who will put any of the items into his mouth.)

Puppets
Make a variety of puppets for your children to play with, creating them from paper, paper bags, socks, gloves (with pom-pom people on each finger), felt, cardboard on Popsicle® sticks. If you wish, you could make puppets to go with recorded stories, and let your child make the puppet act out the story as it is told.

Scout activities
If you have Cub Scouts or Boy Scouts or Brownies or Girl Scouts in your family, have them take their books on the trip. Some of the requirements can be met while you're driving, and your kids will have a real sense of accomplishment at the end of each day.

Finger plays
Do finger plays with your baby and toddler. They'll love it—and so will you. Some common finger plays you may want to do: Pat-a-Cake, Eensy Weensy Spider, and (though not technically a finger play) Peek-a-Boo. If you don't know many finger plays, you may want to check out a book from the library describing the many other fun finger plays parents do with their babies.

Singing Songs—Your Family Chorus

You say you can't carry a tune in a bucket? No matter—it's much easier to carry a tune in a car. When your family sings together, the miles will fly past and you'll have a great time.

Singing is wonderful way to get crabby family members into a better mood and to unify the group. It's a particularly good way to pass the time in the early hours of darkness, when it's too dark to read or draw or play games that require sight, but it's still too early to go to sleep. There are many ways you can have fun with songs on your trip. Here are some suggestions:

- Take your favorite song books along to help you remember the songs you like—and to help you remember the words. You may wish to buy a camp song book or activity song book just for trips.

- Type the words to favorite songs on four- by six-inch cards and take them along on the trip.

- Make instrumental tapes of songs you like and sing along.

- Play a game by humming a tune and having the others guess what it is.

- Try the following: nursery songs, folk songs, camp songs, Christmas songs, singing in rounds.

- Have your children teach you songs they've learned at school.

- Teach your children songs you learned when you were younger.

- Play a game by having the first player sing the first line of a song and requiring the second player to sing the second line quickly and correctly. Continue until the song is over.

- Create variations of well-known songs. For instance, instead of singing "Old MacDonald" in the traditional way, sing "Old MacDonald had a burger." On his burger you can say he had a pickle, lettuce, ketchup, a bun, and so forth. With a little thought, other songs can be adapted to fit with your family or with the trip.

Some Songs to Sing

Some families have great intentions to sing on their trips, but when they get started they can't think of more than a few songs. If you're like that, the following list of popular and commonly known songs will come in handy when you hit the road. (Just remember to take this book with you!)

"I've Been Working on the Railroad"

"Three Blind Mice"

"Row, Row, Row Your Boat"

"Michael, Row the Boat Ashore"

"Ninety-nine Bottles of Pop on the Wall"

"Brahms' Lullaby"

"Hush, Little Baby"

"All Through the Night"

"Mister Frog Went A-Courting"

"Mary Had a Little Lamb"

"Maresey Dotes"

"Twinkle, Twinkle, Little Star"

"This Old Man"

"Eensy Weensy Spider"

"There Was a Little House in the Middle of the Woods"

"The Muffin Man"

"Where's Mister Thumbkin?"

"John Jacob Jingleheimer Schmidt"

"Clementine"

"Bill Grogan's Goat"

"Mulberry Bush" ("This Is the Way We Wash Our Clothes")

"A Tisket, a Tasket"

"She'll Be Comin' Round the Mountain"

"Skip to My Lou"

"The Farmer in the Dell"

"Old MacDonald"

"Are You Sleeping?"

"Yankee Doodle"

"On Top of Old Smoky"

"Alphabet Song"

"My Bonnie Lies Over the Ocean"

"Camptown Races"

"Ten Little Indians"

"Swanee River"

"London Bridge"

"Oh Dear, What Can the Matter Be?"

"Over the River and Through the Woods"

"Won't You Come Home, Bill Bailey?"

"Down in the Valley"

"Do Your Ears Hang Low?"

"He's Got the Whole World in His Hands"

"If You're Happy and You Know It"

"If I Had a Hammer"

"Edelweiss"

"The Happy Wanderer"

"O Shenandoah"

"This Land Is Your Land"

"Greensleeves"

"The Whistling Gypsy"

Books and Tapes for the Trip

How to enter a wonderful world of song and story, traveling from Camelot to the home of the Three Bears—all on one tank of gas!

"Mommy, read me a story."

Who hasn't heard that request? And who hasn't regretted that there weren't more hours in the day to read to a little one?

A trip—which often involves many hours cooped up in a car or airplane—provides a marvelous opportunity for parent and child to read together.

You can take a few favorite storybooks to read.

You can spend some time learning nursery rhymes.

You can laugh together as you try to do tongue twisters.

You can read children's poems, both funny and thoughtful.

You can read a novel to the children—perhaps a chapter or two per day.

You can read books that tell something about the area you're going to be visiting.

Of course, many children will enjoy reading to themselves. But help them watch out for carsickness.

You don't have to <u>read</u> everything to the children. They also like to be told stories that you put into your own words. Don't forget these favorites:

"The Little Red Hen"

"Little Red Riding Hood"

"Goldilocks and the Three Bears"

"The Three Little Pigs"

"Snow White and the Seven Dwarfs"

"Cinderella"

"Pinocchio"

"Sleeping Beauty"

"Rapunzel"

"Rumpelstiltskin"

"Peter Rabbit"

"The Goose that Laid the Golden Egg"

"The Tortoise and the Hare"

"The Lion and the Mouse"

"The Ugly Duckling"

"Ali Baba and the Forty Thieves"

"Aladdin and the Wonderful Lamp"

"Puss in Boots"

"Hansel and Gretel"

"Beauty and the Beast"

"Robin Hood"

"Bre'r Rabbit and the Tar Baby"

"The Wizard of Oz"

"Alice in Wonderland"

"Johnny Appleseed"

"The Gingerbread Man"

"The Ugly Duckling"

"The Emperor's New Clothes"

"Jack and the Beanstalk"

"Tom Thumb"

"The Brave Little Tailor"

You can also tell your children stories from the Bible or from your religious or cultural heritage. Tell them stories from the history of your country or state or province. Kids also love to hear stories of experiences you've had in your own life.

Try a Tape or Two

"I was dreading the trip I had to take with my children," said Carol Lowry. "We had to go from New Jersey to Los Angeles, and I wasn't sure we'd make it through Pennsylvania.

"We packed a bunch of goodies and a pile of blankets and pillows and took off. I had purchased a tape player and headphones for each of my three children, along with a nice box of tapes. I helped the children adjust the volume on their headphones and told them not to turn it up. They obeyed.

"Every other half hour we put away the tape players so they could talk and play games and take naps and eat. And every hundred miles or so we stopped whatever activity we were engaged in, got out of the car, and whooped and ran and stretched our muscles.

◯

"I couldn't believe how the miles rushed past! The kids got tired, of course, but they weren't nearly as crabby about it as I thought they would be. The tapes held their attention the whole time they used them—what happened to the idea that kids have a short attention span?—and our alternating activities seemed to keep them fresh and interested.

"The days passed pleasantly, and before I knew it, we were pulling off our exit at Los Angeles, tired but happy."

Children love to listen and talk to their parents (at least, until they reach a certain age!), but they're also highly captivated by prerecorded tapes. Like Carol Lowry, some parents have taken three-thousand-mile cross-country trips with tapes, and have found that tapes are great trip companions for their kids.

Consider these five ideas with tapes:

1. Get a separate cassette player with headphones for each child. They can then listen to the tape they want, instead of to someone else's choice. But don't forget these two cautions: make sure the volume on the headphones is not too loud, and make sure your kids don't listen to the headphones for a long, uninterrupted period of time. Ignoring either caution could result in permanent hearing loss in your children—and no trip, no matter how quiet, is worth that.

2. Buy storybook tapes for your children, and let them have the visual enjoyment of looking at the book as they listen.

3. Find a radio station in your area that still airs dramatized programs, if there is one. Tape the best programs and take them on your trip.

4. Pull some storybooks from your own shelf and make a tape of yourself reading them. Then take the tape, the book, and the recorder on the trip and let your kids enjoy them on the way.

5. Adults and teens can buy novels and current best sellers on tape, sometimes in condensed versions, sometimes in full.

Brighten Your Day with Brite

One of the best sources of tapes for children is Brite Music, the publisher of this book. Brite Music has excellent cassette programs for families (many with activity booklets) that are great for travel. All are available through your Brite representative. Besides being entertaining and fun and packed with singable songs, Brite tapes teach children important character traits and safety skills. Traveling in a car gives us a perfect opportunity to share learning moments.

Following is a list of Brite's cassette programs, along with ideas on how to utilize them on the road.

1. Standin' Tall®
This is a series of twelve tapes and twelve story/coloring booklets, along with forty-eight stick puppets. With Standin' Tall®, children learn the values of obedience, honesty, forgiveness, work, courage, happiness, gratitude, love, service, cleanliness, self-esteem, and dependability, all through fun stories and songs.

Try these ideas while you're traveling:

- Using Brite's stick puppets, put on a puppet show while listening to the tape. Mom, Dad, or an older child can run the show from the front seat of the car while the younger children sit in the back seat. Or you can give each child a puppet and have everyone be a part of the show.

- On the second side of each cassette, the main character's part is left blank so that your child can say those lines (which are printed in the booklet). Let the children take turns role-playing the main character's part.

- Pass out paper and markers and have the children draw pictures about the stories they are hearing on the cassette.

2. I Have a Song for You

This series contains three volumes: "About People and Nature," "Seasons and Holidays," and "About Animals." These albums build self-esteem and delight children with songs about special people in their lives and the wonders of the world around them. The series includes three songbooks and three activity books.

To use I Have a Song for You while traveling:

- Have a family sing-along, using the songbooks.

- Make up finger plays for the songs.

- Play twenty questions with the songs. Have someone think of a song on a tape and, using yes/ no questions, see who can be first to figure out which one it is.

- Play charades by having someone act out the title of the song. See who can be first to figure out which song it is.

- Play "Name That Tune." Have someone hum the first few notes to a song. The first one to name the title gets to hum the next song.

3. <u>Watch Me Sing</u>
These two tapes (song books also available) provide a great way to get the wiggles out of your young children. All of the songs involve children in activities, many of which can be adapted to the confined area of a car. The music is happy and fun and will keep everyone in a good mood.

One mother says that she played <u>Watch Me Sing</u> for her nine-month-old baby on a twelve-hour trip. He clapped and sang and was happy the entire time.

Try these ideas:

- Many of the songs have hand motions to them. The songbooks give suggestions on what to do—or you can invent your own.

- Have the children use finger puppets (or two fingers) to perform the motions with songs that require running, jumping, or hopping.

- When you're at a rest stop, get out of the car and have the children do the actions to "See Me Run."

4. Safety Kids®
These two tapes combine a lot of fun with some very important safety lessons about the dangers of drugs and how kids can protect themselves from kidnapping and sexual abuse. Your time together in the car may be the perfect setting for a discussion. In addition to the cassette tapes, each includes a coloring booklet. Songbooks are also available.

Here are some ways to use Safety Kids® on the road:

• After playing the tapes, have a question-and-answer time with your children. (Both books have a parent's guide to help you further teach your children about essential safety skills.)

• Have your children memorize the safety rules. Give each child a Safety Kids® badge (available from your Brite Music representative) or some other reward for his accomplishment.

• Play a game of "What would you do if . . . ?" Have one person think of a situation and another think of a proper response.

• Do a readers' theatre. If you like, you can purchase stick puppets, dialogue books, and orchestral accompaniment cassettes from your Brite Music representative.

5. Show a Little Love
Extra love and kindness are definitely needed during fun but stressful vacation times. This tape and songbook will help the children reach outside themselves in love both during the trip and at home.

While you're traveling, try these ideas:

- While your children listen to the tape, have them draw a heart on a paper every time they hear the word <u>love.</u>

- Have everyone tell something they like about each member of the family.

- Draw names for secret pals and do secret acts of service for each other.

6. <u>Take Your Hat Off When the Flag Goes By</u>
(This is marketed to U.S. customers.) Vacation is an ideal time to teach children about their country and the freedoms guaranteed by the Constitution. With this set, including a cassette and booklet, the children can have fun and learn at the same time (Songbook also available).

Here are two ways to use this set while in the car:

- Have your children take one of the quizzes found in the back of the booklet. One is simple and the other more advanced. The answers are found in the program on the tape.

- Have a family discussion about the freedoms the Constitution guarantees us and why each one is important.

7. <u>Brite Dreams</u>
Is it quiet time? Put on <u>Brite Dreams</u>, a tape that contains traditional lullabies as well as twelve beautiful original lullabies. The booklet contains lovely pictures along with all the lyrics to the songs so you can sing along.

The traditional lullabies in <u>Brite Dreams</u> include "All Through the Night," "Rock-a-bye Baby," "Sweet and Low," and "Lullaby and Goodnight." Some of the original lullabies on the tape are "If Babies Were Birdies," "Sandman," "Little Baby Toes," and "Sleepytime Lullaby."

Here are a few lines from one of the songs in <u>Standin' Tall</u>® <u>with Gratitude,</u> by Janeen Brady:

Think about a thank you,

Think about a thank you,

Doesn't hurt a bit to say,

It's not much to give away—

Two little words.

Think about a thank you,

Think about a thank you,

It won't cost you anything,

But it's worth remembering—

Two little words.

Playing Games on the Go

How to let your family's minds soar while their bodies remain confined in the car.

"There's nothing to do," Justin moaned.

"Here, try this new coloring book," Mom offered.

"Nah, I'm tired of coloring," Justin said.

○

"I want it!" Andrea shouted.

"Okay," Mom said, handing the coloring book to Andrea.

"But I need something to do," Justin repeated.

"How about this storybook?" Mom asked.

"Nah, reading makes me sick at my stomach."

"I haven't seen that book," Barry chimed in. "Can I look at it?"

"Okay," Mom said, and she gave the book to Barry.

"But what am I going to do?" Justin whined.

"Why don't you play with the puppets?" Mom suggested.

"I played with them this morning."

"I'd like to play with them," Lori said. "I haven't tried them yet."

"Okay," and Mom handed the puppets to Lori.

"What am I supposed to play with?" Justin moaned again.

"Why don't you play a game with me?" Mom said.

"That sounds fun!" Justin said, perking up.

"I want to play," Andrea said, putting her coloring book aside.

"Me, too," Barry said, putting his storybook aside.

"Yeah!" agreed Lori, her puppets forgotten. So Mom played a game with them all.

It's a good idea to take toys and activities with you on the trip, but often the thing kids want most is human interaction—to play a game with Mom or Dad or each other. Games are the best way of all to pass the time on a trip.

Suit your activities to the ages and abilities of your own kids. When your child turns three or four he will begin to love playing group games, but one-on-one play is more appropriate for children under three.

Rules to Start With

Each game will have its own rules, but you'll want some rules for games in general. Here are four:

1. If children of different ages are playing the same game, give the older ones a handicap, or make the younger child's task in the game easier.

2. From time to time, make the game more interesting by giving the winner some kind of prize—a candy bar, a small toy, or gold stars. Or give points or "lucky bucks" which can be redeemed for a prize or special privilege later. Another approach: don't worry about who wins, and give prizes to all the good sports.

3. Some games work best when the parents get involved. Plan ahead to play with your children, at least some of the time, and all will enjoy it more.

4. When the kids get tired and start to fight, have them try a new game. When nothing works to keep them happy, it's time to stop and let them stretch their legs, or eat lunch, or take a nap.

Before you leave on your trip, you'll want to review the games described below. Some require materials you might not have with you—such as paper and pencils, decks of cards, and dice. And it will be easier to teach the games to your children if you're already familiar with them.

1. Games to Play with Paper

For these games you'll need a stack of sheets of paper (scratch paper is great—you need to have only one side clean) and pencils or pens or crayons.

Round-Robin Drawing. Draw part of a picture, using only the top third of the paper, then fold the paper over so only the bottom portion of the picture shows. Don't let anyone see what you've drawn. Hand the paper to the next child, who makes a continuation of the lines he sees, drawing on the next third of the paper. When he has finished, he folds the paper again, and hands it to the next player.

When the picture has been drawn on all three thirds of the paper, unfold the page and see what you've created.

Homemade Jigsaw Puzzles. Each player draws a masterpiece on a sheet of paper. (Or just draw a simple picture—you choose!) When you're finished, neatly tear or cut each sheet into several pieces. Trade your "homemade jigsaw puzzle" with another player. The winner is the first one to put a puzzle back together again.

Dot to Dot. Each player starts with a clean sheet of paper. Draw fifteen to twenty dots on your sheet, placing them at random, wherever you like. When you're finished, each of you pass your paper to another player.

Now draw a picture from the dots someone else has put down. All players who can create a recognizable picture from their dots earn ten points. If you absolutely must, you can add four more dots to the page—but you'll lose a point for each dot you add.

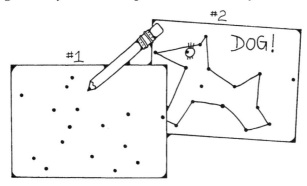

Doodles. Draw a small squiggly line (only one!) on a sheet of paper. Pass the paper to another player, who must draw something that includes the squiggly line in the picture.

○

Question/Answer Scramble. Each player writes five questions on five pieces of paper, and five answers on five more pieces of paper. Put all the questions in one bag and all the answers in another bag. Hold the bags tight and shake them. Then take turns drawing a question out of the first bag and an answer out of the second bag. The results will be hilarious!

Dots and Lines. Start this game by drawing a number of small dots on a page—at least six but no more than ten. Keep them big enough to see well, even when lines are drawn through them. The object of the game is to be the last person to legally draw a line. Here are the rules:

1. The first player draws a line from one dot to another dot, or in a loop from one dot back to the same dot. The line must stop when it gets to the dots; it must not pass through them.

2. After he has drawn the line, he draws a new dot somewhere on the line.

3. The second player then draws another line between two dots, following these rules:

   a) Lines can go any direction and be any shape or size, but they can never cross each other or back over themselves.

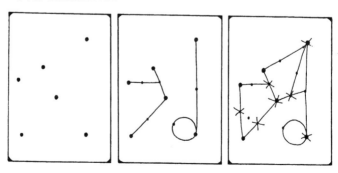

b) Dots must have no more than three lines coming from them.

c) Every time you draw a new line, you get to create a new dot somewhere on it.

Before too long, some of the dots will be "trapped"— you can't draw lines from them without crossing other lines, or the dots will already have three lines coming from them.

The last player to be able to draw a line is the winner.

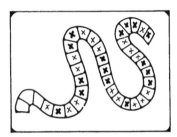

X Marks the Spot. Create a path that meanders across the page, then break the path into squares. The path should have at least twenty squares.

Begin your game by having one of the players mark an X in the first one, two, or three squares. The second player also marks one, two, or three X's. And so on, until you come to the end of the path.

The player who marks the last X in the path loses, so plan ahead!

Memory Test. To play this game, have the first player draw several pictures on a sheet of paper. Draw as many as you can fit on the paper, but be sure to make them recognizable.

Next, show the paper to all the other players for thirty to sixty seconds. When the time is up, cover the paper. The other players are to list all the pictures they saw on the paper. The player who can list the most wins the round.

Boxes in Boxes. Start by drawing a square grid of dots. Put as many dots as you like in the grid, but make sure you have the same number in each row, and make sure you have the same number on the top as on the side.

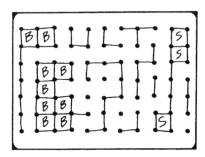

When the grid is ready, the players take turns drawing a short line from one dot to a dot next to it. The lines can be vertical or horizontal, but never diagonal. Whoever creates a small box with his line—by being the last one to draw a line on the box—gets to put his initial inside the box. When you put your initial inside a box, you take another turn.

When all the dots have been used and all the boxes are created, count up all the initials in the boxes. The player with the most initials wins.

S.O.S. This game is played on a grid like Tic-Tac-Toe, but the grid has five (or more) vertical lines and the same number of horizontal lines. Here are the rules:

1. Each player can write an S or an O in any square.

2. The player who spells S.O.S. draws a line through it and gets a point. He then gets to take an extra turn.

3. If you spell S.O.S. twice with the same letter, you get two points—but only one extra turn.

4. If you spot an S.O.S. that someone else created but didn't notice, draw a line through it and you get the point for yourself.

5. When all the squares are filled, the person with the highest number of points wins.

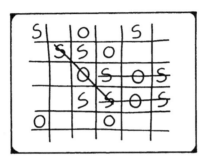

Finger Darts. Make a dart board on a sheet of paper. Start by drawing a big circle. Then draw a circle in the middle and mark it 100. Draw lines, like spokes, from the inner circle to the outer circle. Mark them with numbers for points—but don't choose any numbers higher than twenty.

Now you're ready to play. Put the dartboard on the seat or on a suitcase on the seat. Look at the ceiling (no fair peeking!), circle your finger over the dartboard at least three times, and stab your finger down onto the paper. Mark down the number of points you got. If your finger lands on top of a line, look at the numbers on both sides of the line, and choose the higher number for your points.

Take turns "throwing" your finger darts. The first person to earn 100 points wins.

Squares Within Squares. Each player should draw a grid of squares, eight down and eight across, so that he has sixty-four squares in the grid.

When the game begins, you have fifteen minutes to find and mark the highest number of squares within the larger square. There are at least 204 of them—but it's not enough to know the total. You have to show where they are!

The winner is the player who finds the highest number.

Number to Number.
Write the numbers one to twenty on a sheet of paper. Then write them again, trying to keep matching numbers far across from each other. Hand your paper to another player.

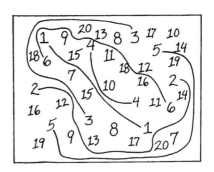

The second player must now draw a line connecting the matching sets of numbers—the first 1 to the second 1, the first 2 to the second 2, and so forth. But wait— none of the lines can touch or cross each other!

2. Word Games

Some of these games require paper and pencil; some can be played with just a voice and an ear. The games that involve just talking and listening are good to play when you're traveling after dark. Of course, they're good for daylight as well.

Forbidden Letter. The players choose a letter (a consonant—be sure not to choose vowels) that is "forbidden"—they must not say any word with that letter in it. If they wish to say such a word, they must replace the forbidden letter with a high squeak.

Suppose, for instance, that you've decided not to say the letter C. The players are required to talk to each other, but everyone must try not to say any word with a C, or to substitute the C in such words with a squeak. When someone slips, he's out for that round.

Player one: "What are the states west of the (squeak)ontinental Divide?"

Player two: "Montana, Wyoming, (squeak)olorado, New Mexi(squeak)o, Arizona, Utah, Idaho, Washington, Oregon, Nevada, Arizona, and (squeak)alifornia."

Letter Scramble. To play this game, each person needs two sheets of paper. On the first sheet, write down ten five-letter words. Then, on the second sheet, write the words again, but scramble the letters.

When everyone is ready, each person should pass his scrambled sheet to another player. Try to unscramble the words on the paper you got, writing the correct spelling of the word next to the scrambled word.

The first player finished with his list wins—if he's correctly unscrambled all his words.

If you come up with a legitimate word that's different from the one your opponent had in mind, you still get credit. Suppose, for example, your opponent started with the word <u>bears</u>, which he scrambled as <u>serab</u>. When you unscrambled it, you came up with <u>bares</u>. Even though it's not what your opponent thought of, you still get credit, since you came up with a real word.

If five letters is too hard for the players, you can try scrambled words of three or four letters. If five letters is too easy, you can try six or seven letters.

In the Trunk. In this game, the players describe a series of fanciful things that can be found in the car's trunk. The first player uses the letter A for his description, the second player uses the letter B, and so on to Z.

As a sample, a game could begin like this:

"In the trunk there's an aggravated alligator."

"In the trunk there's a bald beaver."

"In the trunk there's a cheerful cherub."

"In the trunk there's a dancing dinosaur."

"In the trunk there's an egotistical elephant."

As a variation, you can require the players to remember everything that's been said before them. This game is a little different:

"I looked in the trunk and I saw an aardvark eating an apple."

"I looked in the trunk and I saw an aardvark eating an apple and a blue bear."

"I looked in the trunk and I saw an aardvark eating an apple and a blue bear sitting on a crying cricket."

○

"I looked in the trunk and I saw an aardvark eating an apple and a blue bear sitting on a crying cricket holding a delightful dandelion."

"I looked in the trunk and I saw an aardvark eating an apple and a blue bear sitting on a crying cricket holding a delightful dandelion and an elegant Eskimo."

Backwards Definitions. In this game you choose a word or phrase and give it a backwards—or sideways or opposite—definition. See if the other players can guess what your word is.

For instance, if you want them to guess "horsefly," your clue might be "cowbee." For "Alaska" ("I'll ask her"), you could say, "You'll tell him." For "Good night," you could say, "Bad morning." For "Honeymoon," you could say, "Vinegar sun."

As you can see, this game takes at least as much ingenuity for those thinking up the words and clues as it does for those guessing them.

Secret Letter. A player chooses a secret letter and writes it down where others won't see it. (We'll call this player the "hider," since he's hiding the letter.) The other players list the letters of the alphabet on their papers.

The players ask the hider questions in an effort to get him to reveal what his secret letter is. The hider answers the questions by writing one word on his paper—but he cannot use his secret letter.

The hider must always tell the truth in his answers—unless that will reveal his secret letter. Then he may write something else down.

For example, suppose a player asks, "What is the animal we see at the zoo that's like a horse but has stripes?"

The hider <u>must</u> answer "zebra," unless his letter is Z (or E or B or R or A). Then he can answer whatever he wants—"horse" or "tiger" or "hyena." But be careful—the answer may help to give the secret letter away.

As the hider writes his answers, the other players cross off their alphabet list the letters he uses. Gradually they begin to discover what letter he's hiding.

A player can guess what the secret letter is whenever it's his turn.

Here's how to score the game:

The hider gets a point for every question his opponents ask him, so keep track.

The person to correctly guess the secret letter gets twenty points.

If you guess wrong, you lose five points.

If you have only two people playing, both players will have a secret letter and they'll take turns trying to guess. You won't use the point system, but will simply have a winner of each round.

Geography. The first player gives the name of some geographical feature—a town, city, state, province, nation, mountain, forest, lake, river, stream, ocean, desert, and so forth. The second player must take the letter that the first word ended with and use it as the first letter in naming another geographical feature. If someone can't think of a word to use, he's out until the next round. The last player left wins the round. (Smaller children might use the names of animals instead of geographical features.)

Here's how a game might proceed:

"New York."

"Kansas."

"Saskatchewan."

"Nevada."

"Austria."

"Australia."

"Alabama."

"Argentina."

○

"Atlantic Ocean."

"Niagara Falls."

"Sahara Desert."

And so forth.

Animal Alphabet. Taking turns, each player thinks of every animal he can that begins with the letter A. The last player to think of an animal that hasn't been named wins the round. In the second round the players think of animals that begin with the letter B, and so forth.

Ghosts. The object of this game is <u>not</u> to spell a word. If you do, you start to become a ghost—and everyone knows ghosts can't play games!

Here's how you play:

Step 1: The first player thinks of a word and says the first letter of the word out loud—but he doesn't tell anyone what the word is. (All words must have three or more letters. For older players, you can require even longer words.)

Step 2: The second player takes the letter the first player named, thinks of a word that begins with that letter, and gives the second letter of the word he thought of (but he doesn't say the word itself).

Step 3: The third player takes the first two letters already named, thinks of a word that starts with both of them in order, and says the third letter of the word.

Step 4: If a player can't think of a word that fits with the letters already given, he should bluff by saying any letter that makes sense to him.

○

Step 5: If Player B thinks Player A is bluffing, he can challenge him. If Player A can't give a real word he was spelling, he is out of the round and must write a G (the first letter of GHOST) on his paper. If Player A <u>can</u> give a real word, Player B is out of the round and must write a G on his paper.

Step 6: The player who completes the spelling of a word loses the round and also must write a G on his paper.

Step 7: As play continues, the players gradually spell GHOST on their papers. When a player becomes a GHOST he must drop out of the game. The player left after everyone else has become a GHOST is the winner.

Here's how a game might proceed:

Player 1: "G" (thinking of <u>g</u>ame)

Player 2: "R" (thinking of <u>gr</u>eat)

Player 3: "A" (thinking of <u>gra</u>ss)

Player 1: "V" (thinking of <u>grav</u>y)

Player 2: "E" (thinking of <u>grave</u>l)

Unfortunately for Player 2, even though he was spelling <u>grave</u>l, he spelled a real word, <u>grave</u>. Thus he lost and has to write G on his paper.

Sadman. This is a variation of the game Hangman. The first player thinks of a word (no proper nouns) and marks on the page a number of short lines, one for each letter of the word.

The second player now begins to guess what the word is. Keep track of your wrong guesses on a sheet of paper, so you don't say a wrong letter twice. When you guess right, the first player will write the correct letters on the lines he drew.

Each time you guess wrong, the first player will draw a part of Sadman, who is a stick figure with a face. The parts of Sadman are:

1—first leg

2—second leg

3—torso (belly and chest)

4—first arm

5—second arm

6—head

7—first eye

8—second eye

9—frowning mouth

The object of the game is to guess the complete word before Sadman is all drawn.

You can guess the word any time you like, but if you guess wrong, you'll get two parts of Sadman drawn on the paper.

If you figure out the word before Sadman is completely drawn, you win the round and get one point. If you don't, your opponent gets a point.

Word Scramble. Before leaving on the trip, a parent can make a list of cities, states, and prominent landmarks you'll be passing by or through. Scramble the letters and make copies for the kids. Pass out the copies and have them unscramble the words. The first one finished gets a prize.

As a variation on this game, you can scramble words in a certain category—zoo animals, for example, or farm animals or vegetables or makes of cars.

Double Letters. Take turns naming all the words you can think of that have a double A in them—aardvark or Aaron. The last person to think of one wins the round. Then move on to words with a double B—rabbit, cabbage, cribbage, and so forth.

Category Word Guess. The first player chooses a category (animals, flowers, cars) and lists ten words that fit under the category heading. He then tells the other players what category he's chosen and tells them the first and last letters of each word on his list. The other players guess what each word is.

Players get a point for each word they guess correctly. The first player gets a point for each word his opponents are not able to guess.

If a player guesses a word that fits the category, and has the correct beginning and ending letters, he gets the point even if it isn't the word the first player had in mind.

Multiplying Words. The players choose a word to start with. It should have at least five letters in it—preferably more. Then all the players write on their papers all the other words they can think of that use those same letters. Words listed must have at least two letters in them.

After three or four minutes, stop the game and compare lists. Players get a point for each legitimate word they thought of.

For example, suppose you start with the word <u>travel</u>. That one word could be made into the following words:

let	ale	tale	rave
lave	tar	vat	vale
real	veal	rat	rate

and others.

Verbal ABC. This game is played as follows:

The first player says "A is for apple"—or something else that starts with A.

The second player says "A is for apple; B is for Bird"— or something else that starts with B.

The players go all the way through the alphabet. Each player starts with twenty points. Every time a player can't remember what one of the letters stands for, he loses a point. The player with the most points at the end of the alphabet wins the round.

Transformations. Start this game by choosing two words with an equal number of letters. Each player should write them down on his paper. The object is to transform the first word into the second word by changing the word a letter at a time. Each time you make a change, the resulting word must be a real word.

For example, suppose you start with the word <u>dog</u> and you're going to transform it into <u>cat</u>. Here's how you might do it:

1. dog
2. cog
3. cot
4. cat

The person who makes the transformation using the fewest steps wins the round. The longer the word you're trying to change, the harder the task—so you might want to start with three-letter words before you tackle those with four and five letters.

Word Sandwiches. The group should choose a long word, with six or more letters. Each person should then write it vertically from top to bottom along the left side of the page. They should also write it vertically up the middle of the page, running bottom-to-top, on the same lines as before.

Once the letters are set up, write words that start with the letter on the left-hand side and include the letters on the right. You get a point for each word you can write.

For example, suppose you choose the word VACATION. Here's how your finished game might look:

V a c a t i o **N**

A u t   **O** m o b i l e

C h r   **I** s t m a s

A n o   **T** h e r

T   **A** t t l e

I   **C** k y

O v e r c   **A** m e

N e   **V** e r

If you want to make this game more difficult, require that the word start with the letter at the left and <u>end</u> with the letter at the right.

Word Shuffle. To get set up for this game, have one player write a short, silly story. Meanwhile, all the other players should be making a list of verbs—action words such as talk, eat, chew, drive, chase, jump, run, slide, blink, punch, smile, and so forth. Try to get a lot of variety into your list. After the story is written, the writer should go back through it and circle all the verbs.

When everything is ready, give the list to the person with the story. He is to read the story—but when he comes to the first verb he circled, he should read the first verb on the list instead of the word he circled. He should replace his second verb with the second verb on the list, and so forth.

As he reads, the reader should change the form of the verb to make it work, if necessary. For example, the list might say <u>run</u>, but the reader should say <u>ran</u> or <u>running</u> if it makes more sense.

It's a lot of fun to hear about a "boy who <u>cried</u> down the hill to <u>squeeze</u> a pail of water," or about the "dog that <u>swallowed</u> so loud he <u>dropped</u> the neighbors up."

Category Contest. Write the names of ten or twenty categories on slips of paper and put them in a paper bag. Some good categories might be games, cars, trees, fruit, flowers, TV shows, books, storybook characters, cartoons, songs, sports teams, and so forth. Choose categories that fit the interests of the players. Divide the players into two teams.

Now pull one of the category slips out of the bag. The person that starts first says something that fits with the category, and the next person, on the second team, answers back. They continue going back and forth until a team can't think of a word that fits the category. (Team members can help each other with the answers.) The last team to name something in the category then gets a point, and the play moves to another round by drawing another slip from the bag.

For example, suppose you drew the category of vegetables from the bag. Here's how the game might go:

Team 1: "Lettuce."

Team 2: "Squash."

Team 1: "Cabbage."

Team 2: "Carrots."

Team 1: "Asparagus."

Team 2: "Okra."

Team 1: "Broccoli."

Team 2: "Beets."

And so forth.

Category Chain. Choose a category, such as "animals." The first player names something that fits the category— say, "elephant." The next player must also name something that fits the category, but it must begin with the last letter of the previous word. In our example, the second player might say "tiger." The third player could say "rat," and the fourth could say "tapir." No word may be used more than once.

"I'm Going on Vacation." This is another memory sequence game. The first player names something he's going to take on vacation, the second player repeats the first player and adds something else, and so forth.

For example:

First player: "I'm going on vacation and I'm going to take a change of clothes."

Second player: "I'm going on vacation and I'm going to take a change of clothes and my baseball cap."

Third player: "I'm going on vacation and I'm going to take a change of clothes and my baseball cap and my curling iron."

And so forth.

Any player who forgets the sequence is out of the game for that round. The last one left is the winner.

3. Guessing Games

Note: Some of these games can be played in the dark.

Hul Gul. This guessing game dates back to ancient Greece. Start by giving each player ten "counters"—pennies or small pieces of paper or small pebbles. The first player secretly hides some of his counters in his fist. He then turns to the next player and says, "Hul Gul."

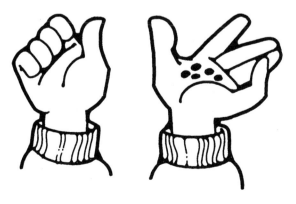

The second player answers, "Handful!"

The first player responds, "How many?"

The second player then must guess how many counters the first player is holding in his hand.

If he guesses correctly, he gets to keep all the counters the player is holding.

If he guesses too many, he has to give the first player the difference between his guess and the real number the first player is holding. (In other words, if the second player guesses nine, and the first player is holding only six, the second player must give three counters to the first player.)

If the second player guesses too few, he has to give the first player five of his counters, unless the second player has fewer than ten. Then he has to give the first player only half his counters. (If the second player has an odd number, say seven, he has to give away only three, the smaller side of the half.)

The player who ends up with all the counters wins the game.

Auto Hide and Seek. The first player writes on a piece of paper a place in the car where he's "hiding." The other players ask "Twenty Questions" to find out where he is.

Button, Button. Divide into two teams, and have all the members of each team sit together. Give one of the teams a button or coin. They secretly shuffle it back and forth among themselves until one of them hides it in his fist. Then they all turn and hold their closed fists in front of them.

Team B then tries to guess where the button is. If they think one of the fists is empty, they point to it and say "Take it away." The owner of that hand then puts it behind his back. If they think a fist holds the coin, they say, "Open up." The owner of that hand then holds it open.

If Team B guesses wrong, they lose the round, and Team A gets a point. Team A also gets another turn. If Team B guesses right, they get the point and they get the next turn.

Twenty Questions. In this game the first player thinks of an object or thing and tells the other players if he's thinking of an animal, vegetable, or mineral. The other players try to guess what it is by asking yes/no questions. They have twenty tries to guess what the first player has in mind. The person who guesses correctly gets a point and gets to take the first player's place in the next round. If no one can guess after twenty questions, the first player gets a point and gets to think of something else for the next round.

Time and Distance. Each time you start driving after a rest stop, pick a landmark far in the distance and ask everybody in the car to guess how far away it is and how long it will take to get there. Mark down all the answers. Also mark down the numbers on your odometer and the exact time.

When you pass the landmark, note the time and the odometer reading again. The people who guessed closest in each category get a point. If one person guessed closest in both categories (time and distance), he also gets a bonus point.

Time Guesser. For this game you'll need a watch with a second hand or with a digital second counter. Designate one person as the timekeeper. He won't be able to play, but he can take turns with someone else after everyone plays a round.

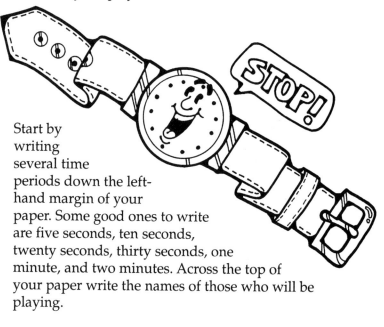

Start by writing several time periods down the left-hand margin of your paper. Some good ones to write are five seconds, ten seconds, twenty seconds, thirty seconds, one minute, and two minutes. Across the top of your paper write the names of those who will be playing.

Now begin the game by having the players take turns guessing how long each time period lasts. For example, if they're guessing the length of five seconds, the time-keeper gets his watch ready and then says "Go!" When a player thinks five seconds have passed, he says "Stop!" The timekeeper checks his watch to see how much time has really passed, then marks the number under the person's name on the paper. If the player said "Stop!" after six seconds, the timekeeper writes "six" on the paper.

After everyone has guessed five seconds, the time-keeper announces how everyone did and tells the player who won in the five seconds category. That player gets a point.

The players then move on to the next level and guess ten seconds.

When they've guessed all the time periods on your paper, total the points for each of the winners and announce the winner of the first round.

Mile Guess. When the driver says "Go!" all the players close their eyes and remain totally silent. When a player thinks a mile has passed, he says "Now!" The player who gets closest wins a point. To keep this game fair, the driver must maintain a constant speed while everyone is guessing.

Rhyme Guessing. The first player says, "I'm thinking of a word. It rhymes with [blank]." The other players take turns guessing. Whoever gets the right answer gets to think of a rhyme for the next round.

4. License Plate Games

"I Have a Secret Word." For this game, each player needs two sheets of paper. On the first sheet, each player should write a secret five-letter word. On the second sheet, write the names of all the other players.

Begin the game by having the first player watch for a passing license plate and call out a letter he sees. "I see an E."

The other players must then answer, "I don't have any E's," or "I have an E," or "I have two E's"—whatever is actually in their secret words.

All the players write down who has an E. If no one has an E, the second player gets to call out a letter he sees. But if anyone has an E, the first player gets another turn.

The object of the game is to be the first person to guess another player's word. You can guess only when it's your turn. If you guess correctly, you win the round.

Spell-a-Word. Put letter slips or commercial letter tiles in a paper bag and let each player pull one out. Players then watch the passing license plates to see if they can spot their letter. The first one to see his letter on a license plate gets to write it down on his paper. Then everyone must return the letters to the bag, and each draws out a new letter.

The first player to accumulate enough letters to spell a four-letter word wins the round. (You can make the game harder or easier for different age players by changing the requirements. A younger player might be required to spell a word only three letters long, while an older player might be required to spell a word five or six letters long.)

○

Fill in the Map. Before you leave on your trip, get copies of line drawings of maps of the areas you'll be traveling through. Pass them out. Then as you see license plates for different states or provinces, color that state or province in on your map.

Find-a-Word. Each player should think of a word or phrase that's at least eight letters long. Write it down on a piece of paper. When everyone is ready, start looking at license plates and signs to find the letters in your word or phrase. You must find them in the right order. For example, if your word is TRAVELER, you must find a T before you can look for an R—and before you can count any R you happen to see.

As you see the letters you need, mark them down under the word you've written.

The first one to see all the letters in his word or phrase, in the correct order, wins the round.

Add It Up. You can play this game in three ways:

1. Take turns looking at license plate. Each person gets to look at only one plate per round. Add all the numbers on the plate. The person with the highest total wins the round.

2. Choose a number, such as ten. Each player picks a passing license plate and adds the numbers on it together. The first player whose plate totals exactly ten wins the round. If no one's plate adds up to ten in the first go-round, continue to take turns looking at passing license plates until someone wins.

3. Give everyone ten minutes to write down ten license-plate numbers from ten passing cars. Try to find the

biggest numbers you can. Once a number has been written down, you can't discard it. And if you don't have ten written down by the time ten minutes is up, you have to use only what you have. When the time is up, everyone adds together the numbers they've written down. The one with the highest total wins.

As a variation of these three games, you can play license-plate multiplication. The rules are the same, except that you multiply all the numbers instead of adding them.

Wipe Out! Divide into two teams. The first team writes the numbers 0, 1, 2, 3, and 4 on its paper, plus the letters A through M. The second team writes the numbers 5, 6, 7, 8, and 9 on its paper, plus the letters N through Z. (If you wish, you can assign the letters differently, since the second half of the alphabet has many letters that are used less often, such as Q, V, W, X, and Z. One way to divide the letters is to have one team start with A and take every other letter as they progress through the alphabet, and have the other team start with B and do the same. So the first team would have A, C, E, G, I, K, and so forth; the second team would have B, D, F, H, J, L, and so forth.)

Once your papers are ready, have the two teams trade them. The object is to find all the letters and numbers on your opponents' paper by watching license plates and signs you pass. Cross them off as you see them. The first team to cross off everything on the page calls "Wipe out!" and they win the game.

If you want to make this game more difficult, have a rule that either team can find only one letter or number on each sign or license plate. The first team to call it out gets it.

Creating Cooties. Be the first kid in the car to draw a cootie and you'll win the game!

Here's how you play.

1. Be the first one to spot a number 1 on a license plate and you get to draw the cootie's body. If someone else spots the plate first, you have to wait and try again. But two different people can use the same license plate for two different numbers.

2. Find a number 2 on a license plate, and you get to draw the cootie's head.

3. Find a number 3, and you get to draw the first eye; a second 3, and you get to draw the second eye.

4. The number 4, found on two different license plates, lets you draw the two antennas.

5. The number 5 will let you draw the cootie's tail.

6. The number 6, found on six different license plates, lets you draw the six legs.

The first one finished with his cootie wins the game.

Message Making. Get your papers ready and have one of the players watch the passing license plates. He will call out the first ten letters he sees, and everyone should write them down in order.

Now it's time for everyone to create a message from the letters they've written down. Use each of the letters as the first letter of each word in your message. Your message will thus be ten words long.

For example, suppose the ten letters you've written down are SDUMKLKWEP. Your message might be something like this: Silly Deer Under My Knees Like Kids With Eskimo Pies.

Your message must make at least a little bit of sense.

When all the messages are written, read them to each other, have a good laugh, then start over again.

Find-a-Number (A). Pick a number, such as 192 or 1920, and look for it on a license plate. Every time you see those digits scrambled up, you earn a point. If you can find it in the correct order, you get five points. And if you can find it in the correct order with no other numbers on the plate, you get a five-point bonus.

The first player to earn ten points wins.

Find-a-Number (B). Choose a kind of number combination you're going to look for on license plates and earn points for finding it. Some things you could look for:

1. Numbers that appear as doubles (the twos in 93221 or the fives in 45503). Each double you spot would earn you a point, if you're the first one to spot it. Numbers appearing as triples could earn two points each.

2. Numbers that appear in sequence (12345 or 76543).

A sequence of three could be worth one point, a sequence of four could be worth three points, and a sequence of five could be worth five points.

3. Numbers that appear as palindromes—they're the same frontwards as backwards (454 or 8778). A three-digit palindrome could be worth one point; a four-digit palindrome could be worth two points.

Of course, all these variations could be played with letters instead of numbers.

Travel Crosswords. Create a grid of squares at least twelve across and twelve down, giving you a total of 144 squares in the grid. Make the squares big enough to write letters in.

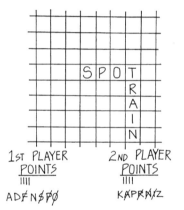

1ST PLAYER
POINTS
||||
ADF N$P∅

2ND PLAYER
POINTS
||||
KAPRN/Z

Now watch for license plates to get the letters you need. The first player writes down the first seven letters he sees. The second player writes down the next seven letters, and so forth.

When everyone has his letters ready, the first player uses his letters to write a word in the center of the grid. He gets a point for each letter he uses, plus a bonus of twenty points if he is able to use all his letters in one turn. When he's finished, he watches license plates again to find new letters to replace the ones he used. He must write down the first letters he sees.

The second player now must put a new word into the grid, using the letters he has written down. His word must go across the first word, crossword style.

115

The player with the most points at the end of the game wins.

Travel Bingo. Each player should make a grid with five squares across and five squares down, making twenty-five squares in all. Inside each square, write a single digit number, from 0 to 9. Don't copy each other, because each bingo sheet needs to be different.

When everyone is ready, assign someone to be the caller. The caller will watch the passing cars and will call out the first digit of a license plate number. Anyone who has that number on his bingo sheet can cross out that square. If he has that number more than once, however, he can cross it out only once. The caller should keep a list of the numbers he has called out, in case there is a question later.

The first player to cross out the numbers on five squares in a row (vertically, horizontally, or diagonally) calls out "Bingo!" and wins the game.

Variations of this game include making bingo sheets with two digit numbers (and the caller names the first two numbers on each license plate), using letters instead of numbers, using the colors of cars and things seen in the scenery, and so forth.

116

5. Observation Games

Count 'Em Up! Divide the players into two teams, and choose something for each team to look for. Team A, for instance, might be assigned to look for cows or Chevys or semi-trucks or black cars, while Team B might be assigned to look for horses or Fords or vans or white cars. Make sure each team is looking for the same <u>kind</u> of thing. Set a time or mileage limit and get busy. The team that spots the most when the time is up wins the round.

Eye Spy. The first player looks around the inside of the car and says, "I spy with my little eye something that is . . . green!" The other players then take turns guessing what it might be, asking the first player only yes/no questions:

"Is it the back of the seat?"

"Is it somewhere in the front seat?"

"Is it the baby's bib?"

"Is it smaller than a foot?"

The first one to guess correctly wins the round and gets to be "it" for the next round.

As a variation, the player can give the letter the thing starts with, rather than its color: "I spy with my little eye something that starts with . . . M!"

Travel Baseball. Get your papers ready to keep track of your score in this fun game.

Each player gets a turn at bat. He watches for cars. A red car gives him a home run. A blue car gives him a single base hit. A black car puts him out. As soon as he's out, another player gets a turn.

When each player has had nine innings (turns), the game is over. The player with the most runs wins.

Scenery, Scenery. In this game, the first player calls out something he sees in the scenery. The second player repeats it, then adds something else. The third player repeats what the first two said and adds a third thing, and so forth. When a player misses an item in the sequence, he has to drop out until the next round. The last player left after the others have dropped out is the winner.

An example of how this game might go:

"I see a tree."

"I see a tree and a bird."

"I see a tree and a bird and a fence."

"I see a tree and a bird and a fence and a cow."

"I see a tree and a bird and a fence and a cow and a blue car."

And so forth.

Cow Poker. Divide the players into two teams, one for each side of the road. Each team keeps a running total of the number of cows seen on their side of the road. They also count white horses—three white horses will triple their score. Thus, if a team has 30 points (from thirty cows) and they see three white horses, their score will jump to 90 points. If they see three more white horses, their score will be 270!

If you see a graveyard on your opponent's side, call "Wipe out!" and they lose all their points.

The teams in one family ended a trip with scores of 96 million to 15, because the team with 15 points had a wipe out only one mile from home.

If you're traveling in an area without many cows (or graveyards), you can find substitutes—different kinds of cars, or signs, or trucks, or whatever works.

Magazine Memory. Before leaving on your trip, cut out a number of pictures from magazines. Choose a variety of subjects, and pick pictures that are both simple and complex.

To play the game, show a picture to one of the players for thirty to sixty seconds. Then ask questions to see how good his observation and memory are:

"How many people are in the picture?"

"What color was the woman's hat?"

"What were the people in the picture doing?"

"What were the three big words at the top of the page?"

Keep track of how many questions you ask, and how many the player answers correctly. Then show another picture to the next player. He should be asked the same number of questions. The player who answers the most questions correctly wins.

"I Spy." Take turns calling out what you see as you travel—but the same thing cannot be named twice. When a player can't think of something new to call out, he has to drop out for the rest of the round. The last player left wins the round.

Race to Z (The Alphabet Game). This game is an old-time favorite. The object is to be the first player to spot the entire alphabet, from A to Z, on signs and on license plates—and to do it in correct order.

There are a number of variations to this game:

1. Make a rule that only the first player to spot a letter gets it. Thus, each will have to call out every letter he sees in order to use it. Or have everyone play silently, and allow everyone to use every letter they see (in the proper sequence, of course).

2. Make a rule that players can use only the first letter of each word they see.

3. Make a rule that all signs are off limits—or all license plates are off limits.

4. Team up younger players with older players.

Truck Count. The players take turns of one or two minutes each and count all the trucks the car passes, on either side of the road. The player with the highest number wins.

If the traffic is not heavy, you may wish to have players count <u>every</u> vehicle you pass.

Scenic Names. Each player should take the first five letters of his name and write them on a sheet of paper. If he has duplicate letters, he should list only one of them and go on to the next letter. Now spend fifteen minutes writing down everything you can think of that starts with each of those letters.

When the time is up, give yourself one point for each item you listed. Subtract five points for any letter of your name that has nothing listed under it.

6. Games with Numbers

A Perfect Ten. Have each of the players create a grid of ten spaces across and ten down. Fill in the grid with numbers 1 through 9, in any arrangement you wish. All the players should have the same arrangement.

1	8	3	6	2	5	4	8	9	2
2	9	6	4	7	1	8	3	4	8
3	7	9	4	1	8	6	5	3	4
2	5	8	3	2	9	4	1	7	3
7	8	1	4	2	3	6	5	9	1
8	1	3	6	4	9	7	5	2	8
8	4	9	7	5	2	3	1	8	1
5	9	4	8	3	2	6	1	5	
1	4	8	2	5	3	6	7	1	
4	2	9	6	4	7	1	8	3	4

When all the papers are ready, give everyone fifteen minutes to circle all the combinations that add up to ten. The combinations must be right next to each other, but they can be arranged vertically, horizontally, or diagonally.

The player with the most correct combinations wins the game.

You may wish to have younger players use numbers from 1 to 5, and have them add the numbers up to a smaller total.

First to a Hundred. Get a sheet of paper and have the first player write down a number between one and nine. Then take turns adding a number from one to nine to a running total. The first player to hit exactly one hundred wins.

"Honk!" Take turns counting, beginning at one and going as far as you can—but every time you come to a number with a seven in it, or a number that's a multiple of seven, you have to say "Honk!" instead of the number. When someone misses, he's out for the round. The last person left is the winner.

An example of how the game would go:

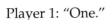

Player 1: "One."

Player 2: "Two."

Player 3: "Three."

Player 4: "Four."

Player 1: "Five."

Player 2: "Six."

Player 3: "Honk!"

Player 4: "Eight."

Player 1: "Nine."

Player 2: "Ten."

Player 3: "Eleven."

Player 4: "Twelve."

Player 1: "Thirteen."

Player 2: "Honk!"

Player 3: "Fifteen."

Player 4: "Sixteen."

Player 1: "Honk!"

And so forth.

7. Card and Dice Games

For these games you'll need either a set of dice or a deck of cards. (In addition to the card games described in this section, travelers enjoy the popular games of Old Maid, Crazy Eights, and Fish.)

Snake Eyes. In this dice game, the only way to score is to get double ones, which are called snake eyes.

Here are the rules:

1. Take turns throwing a pair of dice. Find a level surface to play on, so the dice don't land crooked.

2. If you throw anything that's not a double number, you get no score and your turn is over.

3. If you throw any double number (two 2s or two 5s, etc.), you get another turn.

4. If you throw snake eyes, you get one point.

5. The first player to score ten points wins the game.

Dice Doubles. This is a variation of Snake Eyes. With this game you score every time you throw doubles. When you throw doubles, add up the numbers on the dice to get your points. Then you get another turn.

If you fail to throw doubles, you get no points, and your turn is over. The winner is the first player to accumulate 50 points.

Trickery. Shuffle a deck of cards and deal them out to all the players, reserving one card. Place the reserved card face up in the middle of the group.

The object of Trickery is to get rid of all your cards. Here's how you do it:

1. Look at the card in the middle. When it's your turn, take a card from your hand and place it <u>face down</u> next to the middle card.

2. Go around the circle, taking turns, discarding your cards face down into the middle stack.

3. If you don't have a card that matches the middle one, either in number or suit, you can place down one that doesn't match <u>as long as you don't get caught</u>.

4. If another player thinks you're trying to put down a card that doesn't match, he can say "Trickery!" after you place your card. You must then show the players the card you put down. If you were tricking them, you must add the entire center stack to your hand. But if your card did match the face-up center card, the person who challenged you has to take the entire center stack.

5. After the challenge, the person who picked up the stack must place a new card face up in the center, and the play continues from there.

6. When a player gets rid of all the cards in his hand, he becomes the winner and the game is over.

War. One player deals out all the cards in the deck, giving equal numbers to all players. The players keep their cards in a stack in front of them, face down.

When play begins, all players turn their top cards over simultaneously. The player with the highest card wins all the others.

If two or more players have cards of equal value, a war begins. The players involved in the war place the next three cards from their stacks in the middle, face down, then take another card and place it face up. The player with the highest card wins all the others.

If the cards are equal again, another war takes place. The game continues until one of the players wins all the cards in the deck. If the players grow tired before the game is over (and sometimes War can last a long time), they can stop by counting their cards. The person with the most wins.

8. Other Games to Play

Navigator. Before you leave on your trip, prepare simple maps of your journey for each member of the family. Then, as you travel, have them mark your route on the map with a crayon.

Conquest. To play this game you'll need a map or set of maps. The first player calls out the name of a state or province or country and tells the number of states or provinces or countries that surround it. The other players then have one minute to write the names of the surrounding states or provinces or countries. There is no penalty for guessing wrong, but players must not list more than the number the first player says there are.

When time is up, the player with the most correct answers becomes the conqueror of the state or province or country in question. His name is written on the list of winners, along with the territory he won.

If two players tie, they must flip a coin to see who wins the territory.

Each player serves as caller for four turns, then another player calls for four turns. Play continues until all players have called four times. The winner is the player with the most conquests by the end of the game.

How It's Done. This is a simple game, but it can be a lot of fun. The parents can have the children take turns telling how to accomplish a number of tasks. All descriptions must be verbal—physical demonstrations are not allowed. Some examples of things you could ask:

"How do you make toast?"

"How do you make a burrito?"

"How do you vacuum a floor?"

"How do you wash your face?"

"What does Dad or Mom do to drive a car?"

"How does Dad or Mom mow the lawn?"

"How do you tie your shoes?"

"How do you build a sand castle?"

"How do you eat?"

"How do you make a telephone call?"

Copy, Copy, Copy Cat. In this game, the first player makes three motions with his hands. Then, as the first player begins to make three different motions with his hands, the other players copy the first three motions. The first player continues by making a third set of three motions with his hands, while the other players copy him, always one step behind.

For example, the game might go like this:

First player claps hands three times.

First player circles right fist overhead three times, while other players simultaneously clap hands three times.

First player snaps fingers three times, while other players simultaneously circle right fists overhead three times.

Every time a player makes a mistake he gets a penalty point. When the leader makes a mistake he gets a penalty point and must let someone else become the leader.

When the game is over, all the penalty points are added up for each person. The one with the fewest penalty points wins the game.

Finger Messages. Create a code where each letter of the alphabet equals a number. The simplest code is this:

A1 B2 C3 D4 E5 F6 G7 H8 I9 J10 K11 L12 M13 N14 O15 P16 Q17 R18 S19 T20 U21 V22 W23 X24 Y25 Z26

Now choose one of the group to be leader. His job is to write a little message on paper—which he doesn't show anyone—and then to send the message through his fingers.

He can send the message by counting the first letter of each word with his right hand, the second letter of each word with his left hand, and so forth.

For example, suppose the message the leader wanted to send was "Trips are fun!"

He would start by holding up his right hand and flashing a number of fingers equal to 20. The others would look at their code sheet, see that twenty equals T, and would write T on their papers.

The leader would then raise his left hand and flash 18 fingers, and the others would write down R.

When the first word is finished, the leader should close

his fist and wave it across in front of him, showing that the first word is done and he's going to move on to the next word.

The first player to guess what the message is wins the round and gets to flash a message in the next round.

Rhythm Concentration. This is a fun rhythm game that will wake everyone up.

The rhythm is the undercurrent to the spoken part of the game. The rhythm goes like this: slap both hands against thighs, clap hands together, snap the fingers of the right hand, snap the fingers of the left hand, then repeat endlessly (or until a parent can't stand it any more).

Along with the rhythm of the hands, the players fit a rhythm of speaking, listing things in categories.

Example:

In the rhythm of his hands, the first player will say, "Names of countries." Then, between the clap of hands and the last snap of fingers in the next rhythm series, the second player will say, "Brazil." The next one, in turn, will say, "Cuba." And so forth.

If a player misses his turn or if he repeats something that's already been said, he's out for the rest of that round.

The winner is the last one left.

The Happy Hobo. The players clap and chant in rhythm, "The happy hobo is a [blank] hobo." Each player in turn fills in the blank, using a word that starts with a letter that's been specified for that particular round.

For example, if the letter for the round is B, the players, in turn, might say:

"The happy hobo is a bashful hobo."

"The happy hobo is a beautiful hobo."

"The happy hobo is a bothersome hobo."

"The happy hobo is a blue hobo."

And so forth.

If a player misses his turn or breaks the rhythm, he receives a penalty point. The next player in the sequence then starts with a word that begins with a new letter, and the others must follow suit.

Whenever anyone receives four penalty points, he's out of the game. The last one left wins.

Odd Man In. This is a game for two players. Get fifteen or more small counters (make sure you have an odd number), using coins or toothpicks or pebbles or whatever you wish. Put the counters between you and take turns pulling one, two, or three counters from the pile. When they're all gone, count up how many each player has. The player with the odd number of counters wins.

Cliffhanger. The first person begins a story about someone, but only <u>begins</u> it. After telling a few sentences, he leaves the hero in great danger and turns to the second person.

The second person picks up the story where it left off, rescuing the hero and telling a few more sentences. Then he leaves the hero in new danger and lets the third person take over.

After the storytellers have combined for nine or ten turns, the story should be finished, the hero saved forever, and everyone allowed to live happily ever after. Then, if you wish, you can start again on a new story, with a new hero and a new setting.

"What Did I Draw?" Parents or children can take turns tracing with their fingers on the backs of others. Trace numbers or letters or faces and ask, "What did I draw?" The person on whose back you drew must guess.

Memorizing. A long trip together is a rare time for parents to help children memorize a variety of valuable things. You can help your children to memorize the times tables, the states or provinces and their capitals, poems, scriptures that are important to you, and so forth.

9. Things to Do with Babies and Little Children

Most of the play you do with your baby at home, you can do just as well in the car. Play "Pat-a-Cake" and other finger games, sing songs, and so forth.

In addition, here are a few other ideas:

1. Make little ghosts out of facial tissue or napkins, with a small wad of other tissue in the center and a rubber band around the neck. Draw a face with crayons.

2. Cut out pictures from catalogs and magazines. Staple them together, and let your child look at them on the trip.

3. Point out details in the scenery through the window, telling your child or baby what to look at. Be animated and enthusiastic.

4. Take snap beads on the trip and help your child play with them.

5. Help your child imagine a walk through his room, and have him tell you what he sees.

6. Take little cars and let your child drive them across the front and side of her car seat. Use a car yourself and play with your child.

7. Talk with your child about all the things he did that day.

8. Take a magnetic chalk board, with chalk and magnetic animals or letters, and let your child play with it.

9. Take a variety of hand puppets and play with them with your child.

10. Play a version of "Simon Says" called "Mommy Says," and lead your child through the motions. (But don't do the trickery often used in "Simon Says.")

11. Fill a medium-sized plastic container (with lid) with fun toys for your child to pull out and play with.

4

Time to Be Together

Time to Be Together

One-on-One Talks

How to have a quiet conversation in the front seat while the rest of the family are noisily singing in the back seat.

Thad Marler found a safe spot by the side of the road and pulled over. He glanced over the back seat at his eight-year-old son. "Okay, Scotty," Thad said. "Your turn."

Gina climbed over the front seat into the back, and Scotty took her place. They both rehooked their seat belts. Scotty snuggled close to his dad, and Thad started the car up again.

"So how are you doing, Pal?" Thad asked. "Getting tired of this long drive?"

"Yeah," Scotty said. "But it's okay."

"Tell me about how school's going this year."

"Okay, I guess."

"What's your favorite subject? Do you like reading as much as you did last year?"

"Yeah. I'm reading a good book right now. It's all about a boy who made friends with a fish in a pond near his house."

"What was the fish called?"

"The boy named it Steel, because it looked hard and tough and shiny like steel does. But then he learned it was a girl and he changed the name to Silvery. He thought that was more of a girl's name."

"So what happened?" Thad asked.

"A farmer went out fishing one day and caught Silvery. He was reeling her in and Hank, that was the boy's name, Hank came up just when the farmer was pulling her in. Hank started to cry, but the farmer thought he was just being silly. But when he caught Silvery in his net, she said he should put her back, so he did."

"I'll bet the farmer was pretty surprised when a fish talked to him."

"Yeah, he was. It was pretty funny."

Thad put his arm around Scotty and pulled him closer, speaking very softly. "I've been wanting to talk to you about Gina," Thad said. "You know how she's been teasing you so much and you don't know what to do? Well, I have some ideas I want to talk to you about. . . ."

In this modern age—with eight to ten to twelve hours of work every day, homes and apartments to take care of, grocery shopping to do, cars to get fixed, and on and on—parents rarely have enough time to spend with their children.

When was the last time you sat down with one of your children and spent a few minutes just talking one-on-one?

If you're able to find time often, you're both rare and blessed.

But if those times hardly ever come around, this chapter will be helpful to you. We get too few opportunities to really be with and talk with our children. A long journey provides a ready-made opportunity we shouldn't pass up. It will enable us to give our children the best gift of all: ourselves.

How to Have One-on-Ones

So you're ready to try to find some one-on-one time with your kids on this trip. How can you make it happen?

It need not be hard or complicated. The basic rule is this: pick a child, get him or her to sit by you, and talk.

But, even though that's basically a simple formula, some parents are rusty at it. Here are ten ideas that might help:

1. Both Mom and Dad should have one-on-one talks with the kids—but don't do it at the same time. While one parent is talking with one child, the other should be available to the others.

2. Have the children take turns, either by distance traveled or by time on your watch. If John knows that he's going to get a turn after Mary, he'll be more likely to wait patiently.

3. While you're talking to one child, make sure the other children are well occupied with something else, so you can talk in relative privacy.

4. Have the child sit close to you. Put your arm around him, or put your hand on his knee, or hold hands—somehow convey physically that you love him and that you're glad to be with him.

5. Talk about things the child is interested in. Let him tell you about—

his friends,

his enemies,

his hobbies,

books he's read,

games he likes to play,

foods he likes,

foods he hates,

what he likes about school,

139

what he hates about school,

what he likes about family routines,

what he doesn't like about family routines,

and so on.

Ask questions and listen to the answers. Keep the questions open-ended, so your child will have to answer with more than a yes or a no.

6. Listen with your heart as well as your ears. Listen between the lines. Hear what your child is really telling you, underneath all the obvious words and facial expressions.

7. Be empathetic and nonjudgmental. If your child opens up to you, accept his feelings as legitimate. Talk about the feelings as well as his surface comments.

8. Take the opportunity to bring up things you're concerned about. If he's having problems at home or school or with friends, this is an ideal time to talk.

9. If appropriate, set some goals with your child, to help him to overcome a bad habit or to reach some accomplishment that's important to him. Write the goals down—if you're driving, do it on your first stop—and follow up with your child on a regular basis.

10. Don't end without expressing your love to your child. Tell him how glad you are that he's in your family. Point out some of the things he does well and give him a hug.

One-on-one talks are simple things that can make a big difference in a relationship between a parent and child.

When you're traveling in a car together, the child has a captive audience—and so do you. Taking advantage of it could be the most important thing you do on your entire trip.

"Special moments" with our children are much more likely to occur if we plan for them and if we consciously seek to bring them about. One-on-one talks will help us to do that.

Family Meeting on Wheels

How to take advantage of this unique opportunity to talk with no TV to distract you as you strengthen family relationships and work through problems.

The first official family meeting the Hill family ever had was during a trip from Lubbock, Texas to Houston. They were just outside Fort Worth when the kids seemed to get a little tired of their activities, and Dad could sense it was time for a change.

"Hey, kids, it's time for a family meeting," he said.

"What's that?" asked Lindsay, his fourteen-year-old daughter.

"It's a meeting where we talk about how things are going in our family," Dad answered. "We discuss things that aren't going too well to see if we can come up with some good solutions. And we talk about new things that we'd like to do as a family."

"The Johnsons next door have had a few family meetings," Mom said. "Ruth tells me that the whole family really likes them."

"Even David?" asked Nathan.

"<u>Especially</u> David," Mom laughed. "Ruth says she can't get him to stop talking."

A trip is a perfect time to have a family meeting. After all, there's no phone or television to distract you.When you're traveling in a car, where else are your kids going to go?

A family meeting—

- gives your kids a good place to air grievances and be heard

- provides a setting for your family to settle problems together

- teaches your children how to work together

- helps your family take steps to become better organized

- creates an opportunity for better planning in your family—which in turn will help you more consistently get things done

- gives you an opportunity to teach your children your beliefs and values

- provides a setting where parents can point out good things that are happening in the family

- provides a setting where parents can encourage and build up the children.

Family meetings are most effective when they're held regularly. Many experts recommend weekly meetings. But even if you hold them irregularly, even if you hold them <u>only</u> when you go on trips, they can bring their benefits to your family.

How to Hold a Family Meeting

Whether you hold a family meeting in your living room or in your car, the approaches are essentially the same. You shouldn't make the meeting stiff or too formal, but do have a basic structure, with a few rules to guide you through it. Try these approaches to get started on the right foot:

1. Have communication and agreement as your goal. Use the meeting to build and strengthen your family, not simply as a way for the parents to force their ideas on the children or to discipline specific behaviors.

2. Use the meeting to discuss the following:

- problems that are a matter of common concern to family members

- family plans and activities

- family trips

- good things that are happening in the family

- chore assignments

- beliefs and values

(An example of using a family meeting to plan a trip can be found in the first chapter of this book.)

3. Before you start, have the children help you fill out an agenda sheet. Include all the items family members want to discuss. The agenda sheet will tell you how many things you'll be discussing and will help you to gauge your use of time during the meeting. If your agenda is long, divide it up among several short, pre-scheduled meetings.

4. Let anyone bring up an item of concern for discussion at the meeting. Topics should be limited to those that affect more than one family member;

personal items can be discussed when the child has a one-on-one talk with one of his parents.

5. Assign a member of the family to be chairman, to lead the discussion. This will generally be a parent or an older child. A younger child can take on this task only with much guidance.

6. Assign a member of the family to be a secretary or scribe. The secretary's job is to take minutes or notes of the meeting. That will give you a record for review and follow-up.

7. Consider rotating the jobs of chairman and secretary among the older members of the family.

8. When an item comes up for discussion, let everyone participate, sharing feelings and opinions. Make a rule that no one can judge or criticize or laugh at the expressions of others. In addition, parents should freely use feedback, repeating the child's words or feelings in different words, making sure they understand what the child is saying. Parents should also be careful not to dominate the discussion.

9. Don't let the meeting become a gripe session. One way to avoid this problem is to establish a policy that each complaint must be accompanied with a solution.

10. Use brainstorming to resolve problems.

11. After a problem or idea has been discussed, do not vote on the solution. Instead, see if you've been able to come to a consensus, with everyone agreeing. Voting polarizes, while finding a

consensus unites. If you aren't able to reach a consensus, discuss the problem or idea further—or table it to discuss another time.

12. If appropriate and desirable, spend a few minutes on the family calendar. Record and coordinate activities of the family and of individual members.

13. There are two approaches to ending the meeting. Both work—choose the one that fits your family best. The first approach is to select a set time by which you will end the meeting. Let everyone know when the meeting will end, and then stick by your word.

    The second approach is to let the meeting run as long as the family is cooperating (and you still have things to discuss). But as soon as family members start to act tired or the meeting seems to drag, call it quits. If you still have things to talk about, schedule another meeting.

14. After the meeting is over, you can end on a fun note by playing a game together. Many families also like to have treats after a meeting.

Do family meetings work? Absolutely! Many families find them so useful that they never miss a week.

How about family meetings on wheels? Do they work? Absolutely! You may even decide it was the highlight of your trip.

Air Travel Tips

Air Travel Tips

How to fly the skies and keep them friendly.

"What do you want to do for our trip this year?" Mom asked the kids.

"Fly on an airplane!" her ten-year-old answered.

"Yeah! That's what we want to do!" the others chorused. "Fly on an airplane!"

Traveling in an airplane can be an adventure in itself. In fact, when you fly, your means of transportation might end up being the most memorable part of the whole trip.

Taking a family trip by air is a luxury that many will never be able to afford. Those who <u>are</u> able to go by airplane, however, soon discover that there are definite pros and cons to using such a means of transportation.

The best feature of going by air is the ability to get to your destination quickly. Instead of driving two days to go seven hundred miles, you'll be able to make the entire trip in half a day or less—and that's including time to drive to the airport and from the airport to the motel.

Another advantage, directly related: Flying is a lot less tiring than driving. And a lot more fun for children.

The biggest drawback to flying, besides the cost, is the fact that you and your family are truly cooped up with no escape. When you drive, you can stop almost any time you want if your children are tired and bored and need to run around. When you fly, there's no place else to go. You're stuck.

In addition, you're cooped up with strangers. If you need to discipline one of your children, you'll be doing it with a hundred pair of eyes looking on.

But for many trips, the advantages of air travel outweigh the disadvantages, particularly if you prepare in advance. If you think you might want to make your next trip by air, here is some helpful information to get you going.

General Costs of Flying

In most airlines, a child under two is able to fly free and is expected to sit on his parent's lap. Such infants are not assigned a seat.

On domestic flights, children aged two to eleven (on some airlines, it's two to seventeen) are able to fly at 50 to 80 percent of the standard adult fare.

Airlines are constantly making special offers to attract customers. Once you've decided on your itinerary, call a travel agent and get information on all the special fares available—for adults and for children—from all the airlines that go to your destination. You may save money by having the children fly on one fare category and the parents fly on another. When you make your reservations, ask about family discounts. You may be able to save even more. The travel agent should be able to find all this information for you at no cost to you.

If you're traveling over a holiday, it will be much more difficult to reserve a discount seat. If you must travel on a holiday, you may get a price break only if you reserve your seat far in advance (30 days or more).

Another idea to keep in mind is the <u>triangle or circle fare</u>. As you fly from point A to point C, this fare will allow you to stop at point B along the way with only a minimal charge. For instance, suppose you're flying from New York to Los Angeles, and you decide it would be fun to stop for a couple of days in Chicago or Dallas en route. If your flight already takes you through one of those cities, you can use this fare to add another city to your trip without adding that much to the cost.

Before you purchase your tickets, make sure you know exactly what you want. Changes made afterward can be costly, especially if you've purchased tickets at a special rate.

Choosing the Best Flight

You can save a fair amount of money by flying at non-peak hours. It's generally cheaper to fly—

- during the middle of the week, instead of on weekends

- at night or early in the morning

- when you can fit your trip within the minimum and maximum stay required by a special fare

- when you reserve the tickets and make your payment far in advance

- when you travel in the off season (remember that the off season will vary according to area).

The <u>kind</u> of flight you choose will also make a difference in how well your family weathers the traveling. Here's a quick course in the three kinds of flights the airlines usually provide:

Nonstop. This is the best kind of flight to get. A nonstop flight will literally not stop until you reach your destination.

Direct. This is the second best choice. A direct flight will stop at least once (and often more than that), but you won't have to change planes. You may have a delay at one or more of your stops, however.

Connecting. Avoid this kind of flight if you can. A connecting flight is one where you have to change planes one or more times. Sometimes one airline offers a connecting arrangement between point A and point B, while a second airline offers a direct or nonstop arrangement. Shop around. If you do have a connecting flight, make sure the travel agent leaves you plenty of time to race across the terminal to catch your connecting plane—with three kids in tow.

Making Reservations

You should work out the details of food and seating when you make your reservations.

Upon advance request, most airlines will provide a baby meal, which typically includes cereal, milk, and some jars of baby food, along with spoon, cup, and napkin. They also provide, upon advance request, toddler's and children's meals. A typical toddler's meal would include a peanut butter and jelly sandwich, a piece of fresh fruit, and a small dessert.

The kind of seating you'll want will depend on your needs. Many airlines will provide, upon advance request, a portable bassinet to hold your baby. Such bassinets are usually located on the airplane bulkhead (the wall that separates the different sections of the plane), which would put you at the front of the section.

Here are some other seating tips:

- If your children are sensitive to cigarette smoke, try to be seated at least five seats away from the smoking section.

- Stay away from both the restrooms and the galley. Both areas tend to be busy; other areas will be quieter and make it easier to nap.

- If you're on a movie flight and the film seems suitable, get seats where the little ones can see.

- If your family is large enough that you have to split up, you may want to have the parents trade places in mid-flight to give everyone a change of pace.

- Let your children take turns by the window. That keeps them more occupied and out of the aisles. (But if you find your children are frequently climbing over strangers to go to the bathroom, you may want to move the offenders to the aisle.)

One week before your departure, call your ticket agent to reconfirm your flight plans, including any special arrangements you've made for bassinet, seat assignments, meals, and so forth.

Preparation for the Flight

As with any other part of a trip, being prepared for your flight is the most important thing you can do to make it a success. Here are seven things you can do before the flight to make things go more smoothly:

1. Feed your children before going to the airport. This will make it more likely that they'll sleep during much or all of the flight.

2. Pack a carry-on bag with a few things to occupy your children on the flight:

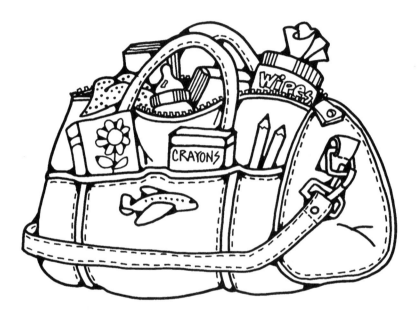

— paper, pencil, crayons and other quiet activities

— a map, to help you identify what you're flying over

— storybooks

— small, quiet toys

— a copy of this book, to use the games section

◇

3. Pack in-flight clothing needs in a carry-on bag:

—a change of clothing for all infants and toddlers

—diaper-changing needs, including extra disposable diapers, baby wipes, and a changing pad

—bibs for infants and toddlers

—pajamas for little ones to wear on long flights— night clothes will help them understand better when it's time to go to sleep

4. Pack food needs in a carry-on bag:

—extra baby food and formula for your baby

—snack foods for older children to nibble on between meals—cheese-and-crackers packs, peanut-butter-and-crackers packs, fruit roll-ups, gum, hard candy, and so forth

—a plastic canteen filled with water so you don't have to bother the attendant or have your child run up and down the aisle every time he or she wants a drink

5. Pack a small carry-on bag for each child to carry. Include in the bag the clothing and activities that child will need for the flight. Or pack your carry-on bags by category: one bag for baby, one for activities, one for clothing, one for snacks, and so forth. (Be sure to find out in advance how many carry-on bags you'll be allowed; airlines typically limit it to one or two.)

6. If you think one of your children is going to get airsick, you may want to give him some motion sickness medication in advance of the flight.

7. If your baby has a cold, give her some decongestant at least an hour before takeoff. If you don't, her

eustachian tubes may become backed up during takeoff, resulting in pain and discomfort.

At the Airport

It's best to arrive at the airport well ahead of schedule. If you can arrive fifteen or twenty minutes earlier than you normally would, you'll do much for your sanity and peace of mind. But before going, call the airline to see if the flight is on schedule.

After you arrive, divide up responsibilities: have one parent check the baggage in while the other supervises the kids. Or you can divide up the children. If the boarding gate is a long way from the ticket counters, one parent can start walking with the children while the other parent checks in the baggage.

If you have a long layover at an airport, you'll want to find some ways to occupy your children:

- Use many of the ideas you use when you're confined in a car or plane—including the scores of ideas in this book.

- Eat at the snack bar, or come prepared to give them snacks from your bag.

- Wander around the airport together looking at the people, shops, and so forth. (Keep your children close, both so they won't get lost and so they won't damage anything in a shop.)

- Let the children make friends, under your supervision, with others who are also stuck in the airport.

- Be aware that letting kids run in the airport often winds them up instead of getting it out of their systems.

Getting Through the Flight

What can you do to avoid any negative aspects of flying with kids?

First, use all the ideas in the other sections of this book that suggest how to travel with children. We won't repeat them all here, but realize that many of the ideas that work for car travel work at least as well in an airplane.

Second, try these ideas that apply specifically to air travel:

- On takeoff and landing, have your older children chew gum to relieve pressure on the ears. Have your baby suck on a pacifier or drink from a bottle. You may also want to place cotton in your baby's ears to cut down on pressure and noise.

- When the newness of flying begins to wear off, ask the attendant for any small toys, games, cards, or pilot's wings he might have for children. The fun things provided by the airline might be enough to keep the children occupied for the entire flight, but don't rely on busy attendants to entertain your children.

- Play games with them, including games found in this book.

- Read stories to them.

- If headphones are available, get some for your children. Ask if the airline has a children's channel. Even if there is no such channel, the other channels will help to occupy the kids.

- If your children get hungry or thirsty, give them some of the snacks and water you brought in your bag.

- When it's mealtime, have the attendant serve your toddler first. After you've supervised him, you can get your own meal—and enjoy it more.

- When it's your children's normal sleeping time, put them in their pajamas (at least the younger ones) and encourage them to go to sleep.

- If you need the attendant to warm up the baby's bottle, she will be happy to help. But warn her of your need as soon as you get on board.

When the flight is over, it may be best to wait quietly in your seats until others have disembarked. Then check under the seats and in storage compartments for all your possessions, making sure you don't leave anything behind. (Also remember to make a similar check in waiting areas and cabs and rented cars.)

After the flight is over, your family may suffer jet lag. To avoid serious jet lag, which can turn into crabbiness and even sickness, try the following:

- Get plenty of rest before you leave.

- Try to nap during the flight.

- Avoid coffee and tea.

- After you arrive, take it easy for the first day.

- Try to go to bed as near normal time (local time) as possible.

Tips for Hotel and Motel

Tips for Hotel and Motel

How to stay in a hotel with four children and have the manager enthusiastically invite you back.

"When we first decided to stay overnight in a motel, we hardly gave a second thought to how our three kids would behave," Harry Dodge said. "They are fairly well behaved at home, and we thought that would translate into good behavior in the motel. It sounded logical. Unfortunately, children aren't always logical."

The story Harry then proceeded to tell was all too familiar to any parent who has stayed in a hotel or motel with more than one child.

"Our problems began in the motel lobby. I had made the mistake of letting the kids come in with me. Our little girl went over to the big potted plant by the window and began to poke in the dirt. The two boys made a beeline for the literature rack, taking three or four of everything they could get their hands on. I made them put most of it back, and we got out of there as fast as we could.

"We went to our room and took a quick survey, and then Penny (my wife) and I went back out to the car to get our luggage. While we were gone, all three kids went wild. The boys were having a grand old time jumping back and forth between the two beds, and they had turned the television on full blast. Little Audrey was sitting on the floor by the door crying.

"I almost grabbed them and headed for home right then. I'd had it.

"But I decided to give everyone another chance. Maybe the problems were my fault, I thought. Here they were in new and exciting surroundings, and I had failed to give them adequate guidance on how to behave.

"So we all sat on the edges of the beds, facing each other, and had a good long talk. My boys are six and eight, so they can't understand everything a teenager would, but they did pretty well. I told them that the motel room wasn't ours, that the motel people were just letting us use it for the night. We were to take extra

good care of everything in the room, I said, including the beds, the floor, the curtains, the table and chairs, the TV—everything.

"Then I talked to them about the other people in the motel—how they had come here to rest and how we needed to stay quiet so they could sleep.

"Finally, I told them that if they were really good for the rest of the night, I'd buy them a special treat for breakfast the next morning.

"They still were a little too excited, and they had some difficulty going to sleep. But they did much better after our talk—and they earned their special breakfast treat."

If you're going to stay in a hotel or motel, one of the best things you can do is let your children know exactly what you expect. Then follow through with the same discipline techniques that work for you at home.

Considerations

Many motels and hotels will let children stay free—some up to age twelve, some sixteen, some eighteen. You'll save a lot of money by going to the trouble of finding such a place.

If you can, make your reservations in advance. That will save you some stress and worry when you arrive at your destination. Be sure to confirm any and all reservations before you leave home, and be sure to make arrangements for them to hold your room if you'll be <u>arriving after six p.m.</u>

Find a place with a swimming pool; your kids will thank you forever.

If you need a crib or cot, ask in advance. Otherwise you may end up without one. And be aware that, because of insurance costs, many motels and hotels no longer provide cribs for their patrons.

If possible, get ground-floor accommodations, and try to get a room that's just off the parking lot. That will save you a lot of trouble unloading and reloading the car. Another advantage of a ground-floor room: you won't have to worry that the noise of your children's running and stomping across the floor will bother someone underneath you.

As soon as you get into your room, unpack your things (unless you're staying only one night—then you might want to live out of your suitcases). Filling up the dressers and closets with clothing makes everyone feel more comfortable and more at home.

To avoid feeling cramped and restless, spend as little time as possible in your room. You haven't gone on your vacation to sit in a room. Use it only as a base when you need to rest or sleep.

If you're in a rented house or condominium or cabin, share the chores with all the kids, giving each a job to do. Or put everyone to work jointly, with all working until all the work is done.

If there is the slightest possibility that one of your children might wet the bed, take a piece of plastic or rubber to put between the bottom sheet and the mattress. This precaution will save you embarrassment and maybe some extra charges from the motel. (One family reports using a large plastic garbage bag on their trips. It works great!)

When you're ready to leave, load everything into the car, then do a last-minute check of all the rooms you've been using, making certain you haven't misplaced or forgotten anything. Check in dresser drawers, under beds, under bedding (if piled), under desks and chairs, in closets, in the bathroom, behind doors and draperies, and so forth.

Room Arrangements

There is nothing sacred about the way the hotel or motel room has been arranged. You should feel free to rearrange things if you see a way to better meet your needs. Just don't damage anything in the process—and don't move anything that's permanently fixed in place! For example, if you should find

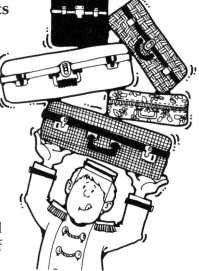

yourselves with fewer beds than bodies, you can move a mattress onto the floor and make an additional bed on the box springs.

One caution: Fire codes limit the number of people you can sleep in one hotel/motel room. Find out what the code is for the city where you're staying, and abide by it.

Also, be completely honest and open with the hotel/ motel desk clerk about the size and makeup of your group. A clear conscience will help you sleep better.

Further ideas on making your accommodations fit:

- Pull a dresser drawer out and set it on the floor, line it with blankets, and put your baby in it.

- If you're worried that someone might fall out of bed, push the bed against the wall and set chairs against the open side.

- Keep your clothing and other stuff well organized in the room. A messy room soon seems much smaller than it really is.

- If you don't have enough beds for everyone, have the kids take turns on the floor. Otherwise, someone is going to feel picked on.

- If you have a large family, consider two attached rooms. One family puts all the kids in one room and the parents in the other, leaving the door between the two partly open. "I can't sleep in the same room with my kids," the mom explains. Another family puts Dad and the boys in one room, Mom and the girls in the other.

Hotels and Food

Many hotels and motels have restaurants that serve their customers as well as the general public. Such restaurants are convenient and sometimes are reasonably priced, but if you're traveling on a budget, you may be in the market for some different ideas:

For instance, if you rent a room with a kitchenette, and if you prepare some of your meals there, your savings can be significant. In making your decision, don't just compare food cost in the kitchenette to food cost at the restaurant. Remember to work in the additional cost of renting a room with an attached kitchen, and don't forget the extra work Mom or Dad will have to do to fix those meals. Even after considering all these factors, you may still come out ahead with a kitchenette.

Often on trips we eat breakfast in the motel room even if there is no kitchenette. We stop at the grocery store and buy milk, a couple of boxes of cold cereal, plastic or paper bowls, and plastic spoons. Sometimes we also buy cinnamon rolls to round out the meal. Everybody gets plenty to eat and it costs little more than eating breakfast at home.

Finally, kids will get hungry between meals in a motel or hotel just as they do at home. If you keep some snack foods in the room, you'll be able to satisfy growling stomachs without spending a fortune at the vending machine.

Crowd Control

One of the biggest challenges of staying in a hotel or motel is getting the kids to settle down. Staying at a hotel or motel is part of the adventure for children, and they seem to want to get the most out of it.

But you don't have to spend the entire time worrying about your children. Try these methods of crowd control:

- Explain all the rules to your children ahead of time—

  no running in the halls

  no noise in the halls

  no loud talk in the room

  no loud TV

  be polite and thoughtful of other people

  no jumping on the beds or furniture—just like at home

- Assign each older child a "Bitty Buddy." Big buddies are to stay with their Bitty Buddies and watch out for them.

- Parents should personally watch little ones in the pool. For further safety and peace of mind, consider life jackets.

- Don't go into the experience expecting to be uptight. Let your children explore the room and have quiet fun. Matthew T. found 101 uses for the luggage stand, and let his tired mom have a nice rest in the process.

- If your children wrestle around on the bed too much when they're supposed to be going to sleep, set some pillows down the middle of the bed and forbid them to cross.

- Read your children bedtime stories when you put them to bed. And try to go to bed earlier than usual yourself: Doing so will help your children to settle down quicker and will allow you to be more refreshed when they wake you up too early the next morning.

- Another way to help your children go to sleep: turn off the room lights, turn on the bathroom light, and sit in the doorway and read by the bathroom light. Be firm about your children staying quietly in bed. When they're asleep, you can probably turn on a lamp and turn the TV on low.

An overnight stop will add a lot of fun to your trip. It will be still another adventure for your children. But if you don't plan ahead, with realistic rules and expectations, you might end up with baggy eyes and a deep sense of exhaustion the next day.

So plan ahead. And have a great time with your kids!

SECTION

How to Make the Same Trip Appeal to Tots and Teens

How to Make the Same Trip Appeal to Tots and Teens

How to meet the fascinating challenge of different ages and different interests while having loads of fun in the process.

The Great Challenge

Fifteen-year-old Brent wants to go backpacking in the Cascade Mountains for the family vacation. Eight-year-old Carma wants to visit Grandma.

Eighteen-year-old Shauna wants to see some of the Civil War sites she's been learning about in an exciting history class. Twelve-year-old Karen wants to go camping.

Sixteen-year-old Wendy wants to spend the entire time on the beach. Seven-year-old Dan wants to spend the entire time at Disneyland.

It's not hard for a family to reach a consensus on what to do when most of the kids are the same age. But what happens when the kids are widely separated by age and interests?

That presents a great challenge in planning a family trip. What works for one age group may not work for another. The key, then, is this: Plan a variety of activities, so everyone has a personal adventure at least part of that time. Or, if possible, plan a single activity that will appeal to all.

If some or all of your children are still quite young, you might do well to save the really big trips—the drive-across-America trips, the ocean-cruise trips, the getaway trips to Europe—until they're older and able to appreciate it better.

But there is still plenty you can do. If you know your kids, you'll know what interests them—and what will work for the entire family as a group. View your trip as an extension of everyday life. What works for you from day to day will give you a helpful indication of what will work on your trip.

Some families have had success in going on vacation to a given area and then splitting up some of the time. On Monday, for example, Dad might take the younger children somewhere while Mom takes the older kids. On Tuesday and Wednesday everybody does something together. On Thursday, Mom takes the young ones and Dad takes the older ones.

A Few Traveling Tips

Children almost invariably get on one another's nerves when they're cooped up together in a car. That potential for conflict is often heightened by mixing together children of several ages. Even two kids can be difficult.

How can you maintain some semblance of peace when your children get tired and bored?

A few suggestions:

- Pay careful attention to the ideas in the chapters on comfort and having fun on the way. That will nip most problems in the bud.

- If problems arise, give the children seating assignments, separating the troublemakers. You may need to have one of the parents sit in the back seat.

- Set up a buddy system, where each older child is assigned to watch out for a particular younger child.

- Take toys and games that hold interest for a broad range of ages.

- Take plenty of paper and pencils, which are fun for kids of all ages.

- Take a variety of books for all ages.

- If the kids start to fight, let them resolve it themselves if possible.

- Occupy an older child by assigning him to help you navigate.

- If you have a child who doesn't have a companion among his siblings, consider inviting a friend to come on the trip with him.

Understanding Your Kids

Every age-group has its own needs. To help you plan and carry out a trip that will be fun for all, keep these in mind:

<u>Birth to age one</u>: Will sleep a lot. You'll be somewhat limited in what you can do. Don't forget to bring all the paraphernalia a baby needs.

<u>Ages one and two</u>: Won't want to stay in her seat. Will make messes a-plenty. Will tag along on just about any activity, but plan on early fatigue, so don't forget naps. And if you're walking around much, you'll probably end up carrying her or pushing her in a stroller.

Ages two and three: More trouble with seat belts, unless she's well trained. More messes, more fatigue, continued need for naps. Also more curiosity and more fun. Need to stop often for bathroom or to stretch legs. Likes finger plays and musical activities.

Ages four and five: Very active and won't want to sit still. Short attention span. Experiences mood swings. Provide a variety of experiences to keep her busy. Likes to pretend and use puppets.

Ages six and seven: Still very active. Growing attention span. Enjoys using small muscles, doing coloring, writing, molding clay. Likes listening to stories and, usually, reading simple stories to others.

Ages eight and nine: Still active but more controlled. Likes organized games. Prefers participation to observation. Can be silly and giggly. Prefers reality to fantasy.

Ages ten, eleven, and twelve: This is the age when girls begin to mature faster than boys. Both can be touchy and irritable, selfish and rude—but also can be serious, thoughtful, and sincere. Both desire increased independence. Boys, this age particularly, like to tease.

Age thirteen and up: The time of painful puberty, agonizing adolescence. This can be a difficult time for parents and children alike. The children can be quite insistent on their need for independence from the parents, and they can be quite outspoken, even rude, in their efforts to demonstrate that independence. They might resist every vacation idea anyone else would like, just to be contrary. They might be sullen or rude in the car. Or they might surprise you and be wonderful angels.

How do you deal with a teenager on a trip?

First, find activities that appeal to teenagers. Better yet, have them propose what they would like to do. If their ideas are reasonable, incorporate them.

Second, give the teen more responsibility. Have her participate in planning the trip, even more than younger kids do. Give her some fun duties on the way—running in to the store for some groceries, acting as navigator, and so forth.

Third, encourage the teen to play with and enjoy the younger children.

Fourth, parents can play games with and enjoy the teen.

Fifth, use all the wonderful techniques you've worked out at home to get along with your teen. (If you feel you need help in that area, you may want to see one or more of the following: Fitzhugh Dodson, How to Discipline with Love, Signet, 1978; Haim Ginott, Between Parent and Teenager, Avon, 1969; and Thomas Gordon, Parent Effectiveness Training, Plume, 1975.)

101+ Tips for a
Great Trip

101+ Tips for a
Great Trip

Throughout this book we've given you scores of ideas for taking great trips with your kids. Now, in this section, we're bringing all of those ideas together, to help you review them and to better use them in your own family.

We're listing the ideas in the same order in which they appear in the main body of the book. For more details on each one, see the appropriate section.

You'll notice as you go through this section that we've given you the promised 101 tips and then many more besides. **As you read this section, watch for the** DOLLAR SAVER! **tips we've also given you.**

□

Section 1: Before You Go

Planning the Trip

1. When you involve your whole family in planning the trip, everyone will be more excited about it.

2. If you need to limit the options, do so at the very beginning, to avoid later disappointments.

3. Plan activities that will best meet the needs and interests of all concerned.

4. A good time to plan the trip is in one or more family meetings.

5. Share the load of planning by making assignments to family members.

6. Get information from the library, from auto clubs, from chambers of commerce, and from specific attractions you wish to visit.

7. Pull all the information into one place where the family can review it together.

8. Plan a variety of activities for each day, especially if you have smaller children.

9. Avoid taking whirlwind tours.

10. Find a central location that you can call "home" during your trip and plan day trips from there.

11. If, after you're underway, you find that no one's having fun, don't hesitate to change the plan.

Earning Your Way Together

12. The more your children put into earning their own way, the more they'll appreciate the trip.

13. Older kids can earn money by getting regular part-time jobs.

14. Younger children can earn money by doing extra work around the house.

15. Kids can also earn money by being entrepreneurs in the neighborhood. (See the list of money-making ideas in the chapter—these DOLLAR SAVER! tips are for the family as a whole.)

Getting Prepared

16. The more you prepare in advance, the less harried and frustrated you'll be when it's time to leave on the trip.

17. Before you leave, remember to use the checklist of things to do to get ready.

18. Create a master checklist of things to take care of and use it for each trip.

19. Delegate some of the preparation tasks to others.

20. If you're going to be visiting restaurants or museums on your trip, have your children practice good behavior at home.

Things to Take

21. Make a master list of things to take on trips and use it over and over again.

22. Plan to have clothing do double duty—for example, only one coat and one pair of shoes per person, if possible.

23. Take clothing that can be worn in several different combinations.

24. Take clothing that can be layered.

25. Take clothes that will require the least amount of care.

Tips for Packing

26. Remember that <u>how</u> you pack is almost as important as <u>what</u> you pack.

27. The children can help in the packing chores, depending on their age.

28. Use one or more of the packing ideas found in the chapter.

29. If you have to use a laundromat while on the trip, let one parent take care of the laundry while the other takes the kids off to do something else.

30. In packing the car, leave easy access to food, water, diapers, games.

31. Keep available a change of clothes for little ones who might have an accident of some kind.

32. As you travel, make a count of your suitcases every time you move them.

□

Preparing Your Home

33. If you get your house ready for your trip, you'll have more peace of mind while you're gone.

34. Take the time to clean your house—at least the surface clutter—and you'll feel a lot better about coming home.

35. Clean out the refrigerator and give perishable items to a friend or neighbor.

36. Don't forget to flush the toilets just before leaving.

37. Use the Checklist for Preparing Your House. It reminds you of things you'll want to do before you leave, including DOLLAR SAVER! tips.

Section II: Comfort on the Way

Comfort in the Car

38. To increase comfort while traveling, limit the number of hours you drive each day.

39. Take time to enjoy the sights along the way.

40. Plan your use of space in the car so everyone will be comfortable.

41. Place the luggage so it won't be in the way.

42. If possible, get a car with air conditioning for summer travel, and make sure the heater works for winter travel.

43. | DOLLAR SAVER! | If you have no air conditioning, buy a small auto fan.

44. Provide sunglasses for everyone in the car.

45. Wear comfortable clothing—loose so circulation isn't restricted, layered so the child won't get too cold or hot.

46. Make frequent rest stops.

Safety in the Car

47. Remember that <u>nothing</u> is more important than the safety of the travelers.

48. Observe the rules of safety discussed in the chapter.

49. Get the kids to wear their seatbelts by: wearing your own seatbelt,

50. starting with seatbelts from the moment they outgrow the carseat,

51. wearing seatbelts even on short trips around home,

52. making sure the child can see out the window with the seatbelt on,

53. never starting the car unless everyone has a seatbelt on,

54. giving the children a reward for wearing a seatbelt without being reminded,

55. pulling off to the side of the road if someone takes his or her seatbelt off.

□

Your Own Rules for the Road

56. Set rules for travel behavior and make sure everyone understands them.

57. The wise use of rewards and punishments will encourage your kids to make good choices.

Food on the Way

58. Eating on the trip will keep mouths quiet and hands busy.

59. See the chapter for tips on preparing before you go (including some DOLLAR $ SAVER! ideas).

60. See the chapter for hints for DOLLAR $ SAVER! meals.

61. See the chapter for ideas on ways to be creative with food (including some DOLLAR $ SAVER! tips).

62. Watch out for sticky foods, sweet drinks, sugar, caffeine, salty foods, foods with strong smells.

63. See the chapter for DOLLAR $ SAVER! ideas for food and drink.

64. Don't forget a jug of water.

Car Sickness and Sickness on the Way

65. Car sickness is caused by confinement, motion, heat, and/or food that doesn't agree.

66. See the chapter for ways to prevent and deal with car sickness.

67. Have a "car-sickness bag" handy just in case.

68. Avoid other sickness on the way by making sure your kids are up to date on their physical checkups, and

69. by getting enough sleep and good nutrition before the trip, and

70. by keeping the family away from communicable diseases before and during the trip.

71. If your child is getting sick just before you leave, you may need to postpone the trip.

72. Take with you any medicines you might need for common ailments.

Section III: Fun on the Way

Setting the Stage for Fun

73. Remember that the more you <u>prepare</u> for fun on the way, the more enjoyable your trip will be.

74. If you provide for a variety of fun activities, you'll be able to keep your kids occupied for longer periods of time.

75. Use the element of surprise, keeping your kids guessing.

76. Good timing is critical. Plan two or three activities per hour.

77. Alternate one type of activity with a different type.

78. Make "activity holders" to hold fun things for your kids to do. (See the chapter for ⌐DOLLAR 🌀 SAVER!¬ ideas with "activity holders").

Toys and Activities

79. Take toys that can be played with in a small space, that don't make a mess, and that aren't dangerous in a car. (See the chapter for types of toys that are fun on a trip.)

80. Let your children make a scrapbook of memorable activities on the trip.

81. Encourage your children to keep a trip journal.

82. Teach macrame while you're traveling.

83. ⌐DOLLAR 🌀 SAVER!¬ Let your children listen to homemade tapes.

84. Have your children send postcards.

85. Let your children keep track of the miles with "travel beads."

86. Let little ones play sorting games.

87. Let your children play with a variety of types of puppets.

88. Have your kids do Scout activities.

89. Do fingerplays with babies or toddlers.

□

Singing Songs—Your Family Chorus

90. Use singing to help get everyone in a better mood.

91. Use singing as detailed in the chapter.

92. Sing some of the favorite songs listed in the chapter.

Books and Tapes for the Trip

93. Pass the time by reading books to each other.

94. Tell your children some of the stories listed in the chapter.

95. Take tapes of songs and stories for your children to listen to.

96. Let your children listen to the many fun tapes produced by Brite Music.

Playing Games on the Go

97. Games that enable the children to interact with their parents and with each other are among the best of all ways to pass the time.

98. See the chapter for general tips on playing games.

99. Games with paper begin on page 84.

100. Word games begin on page 90.

101. Guessing games begin on page 105.

□

BONUS: We promised 101 tips for a great trip, and we've delivered. Now here are many more.

102. License plate games begin on page 109.

103. Observation games begin on page 117.

104. Games with numbers begin on page 122.

105. Card and dice games begin on page 123.

106. "Things to Do" with babies and little children begin on page 131.

Section IV: Time to Be Together

One-on-One Talks

107. A family trip provides an opportunity to spend some time visiting with each of your children, one-on-one.

108. See the chapter for ways to make the most of one-on-one talks.

Family Meeting on Wheels

109. A family meeting is a great way to strengthen the family and work through family problems and concerns. And a family trip is a great time to have a family meeting.

110. See the chapter for ways to make the most of family meetings.

□

Section V: Air Travel Tips

111. Traveling in an airplane can be an adventure in itself.

112. [DOLLAR$SAVER!] Use one of the ideas in the chapter for saving money on fares.

113. [DOLLAR$SAVER!] Use one of the tips in the chapter on when to fly.

114. If possible, save worry and frustration by arranging a flight that has no stopovers and no changes of planes.

115. Make arrangements for seating and special food needs when you make your reservations.

116. See the chapter for tips on seating.

117. One week before your departure, call your ticket agent to confirm your flight plans, including any special arrangements you've made.

118. See the chapter for ways you can prepare in advance to make the flight go more smoothly (including [DOLLAR$SAVER!] tips).

119. Arrive at the airport fifteen or twenty minutes earlier than you normally would—your children will slow you down some.

120. Divide up responsibilities at the airport.

121. See the chapter for ways to pass the time if you have a layover in the airport.

122. See the chapter for things to do in the air to keep your children comfortable and occupied.

123. When the flight is over, it may be best to wait in your seats until others have disembarked. Then check all around to make sure you're not forgetting anything.

124. See the chapter for ways to avoid jet lag.

Section VI: Tips for Hotel and Motel

125. Before you stay in a hotel or motel, let your children know exactly what you expect from them. Then follow through with the same discipline techniques that work at home.

126. See the chapter for ideas for making the most of your accommodations.

127. Feel free to rearrange the furniture to meet your needs. Just be sure you don't damage anything. See the chapter for ways to adjust the accommodations to your needs.

128. DOLLAR $ SAVER! Many hotels and motels will give you permission to sleep your children on the floor.

129. DOLLAR $ SAVER! You may save food costs if you rent a room with a kitchenette.

130. DOLLAR $ SAVER! Buy ready-made breakfast foods at the grocery store and eat in the room.

131. DOLLAR $ SAVER! Buy snack foods at the grocery store instead of using the hotel vending machine.

132. See the chapter for tips on "crowd control" in a hotel or motel.

Section VII: How to Make the Same Trip Appeal to Tots and Teens

133. If you have children of widely different ages and/or interests, plan a variety of activities on your trip. Or find one activity that will appeal to everybody.

134. On some days, you might want to split your family up, with Dad taking some of the kids one direction and Mom taking the other kids somewhere else.

135. See the chapter for ways to help keep peace in the car when you have children of widely different ages.

136. You'll do better with your children if you understand the interests and abilities of each age group. See the chapter for a refresher.

137. See the chapter for suggestions on ways to deal with a teenager on a trip.